HOW TO READ HUMAN NATURE

HOW TO READ HUMAN NATURE:

ITS INNER STATES AND OUTER FORMS

By

WILLIAM WALKER ATKINSON

WITH NUMEROUS ILLUSTRATIONS

GYAN

Published by

GYAN

Gyan Publishing House
5, Ansari Road
Daryaganj, New Delhi-110002
Phone: 011-47034999, 9811692060
E-mail: books@gyanbooks.com

Distribution Network
gyanbooks.com
India, USA, Canada, UK, Australia, France

ISBN : 978-81-212-6340-5 (PB)
First Published, 1916

2nd Impression 2022

Printed at: Gyan Press, Delhi.

HOW TO READ HUMAN NATURE
Author: WILLIAM WALKER ATKINSON

HOW TO READ HUMAN NATURE:

ITS INNER STATES AND OUTER FORMS

By WILLIAM WALKER ATKINSON

WITH NUMEROUS ILLUSTRATIONS

L. N. FOWLER & CO.
7, Imperial Arcade, Ludgate Circus
London, E. C., England

1916

CONTENTS

CHAPTER I

INNER STATE AND OUTER FORM

"Human Nature" is a term most frequently used and yet but little understood. The average person knows in a general way what he and others mean when this term is employed, but very few are able to give an off-hand definition of the term or to state what in their opinion constitutes the real essence of the thought expressed by the familiar phrase. We are of the opinion that the first step in the process of correct understanding of any subject is that of acquaintance with its principal terms, and, so, we shall begin our consideration of the subject of Human Nature by an examination of the term used to express the idea itself.

"Human," of course, means "of or pertaining to man or mankind." Therefore, Human Nature means the *nature* of man or mankind. "Nature," in this usage, means: "The natural disposition of mind of any person; temper; personal character; individual constitution; the peculiar mental characteristics and attributes which serve to distinguish one person from another."

Thus we see that the essence of the *nature* of men, or of a particular human being, is the *mind,* the mental qualities, characteristics, properties and attributes. Human Nature is then a phase of psychology and subject to the laws, principles and methods of study, examination and consideration of that particular branch of science.

But while the general subject of psychology includes the consideration of the inner workings of the mind, the processes of thought, the nature of feeling, and the operation of the will, the special subject of Human Nature is concerned only with the question of character, disposition, temperament, personal attributes, etc., of the individuals making up the race of man. Psychology is general—Human Nature is particular. Psychology is more or less abstract—Human Nature is concrete. Psychology deals with laws, causes and principles—Human Nature deals with effects, manifestations, and expressions.

Human Nature expresses itself in two general phases, i.e., (1) the phase of Inner States; and (2) the phase of Outer Forms. These two phases, however, are not separate or opposed to each other, but are complementary aspects of the same thing. There is always an action and reaction between the Inner State and the Outer Form—between the Inner Feeling and the Outer Expression. If we know the particular Inner State we may infer the appropriate Outer Form; and if we know the Outer Form we may infer the Inner State.

That the Inner State affects the Outer Form is a fact generally acknowledged by men, for it is in strict accordance with the general experience of the race. We know that certain mental states will result in imparting to the countenance certain lines and expressions appropriate thereto; certain peculiarities of carriage and manner, voice and demeanor. The facial characteristics, manner, walk, voice and gestures of the miser will be recognized as entirely different from that of the generous person; those of the coward differ materially from those of the brave man; those of the vain are distinguished from those of the modest. We know that certain mental attitudes will produce the corresponding physical expressions of a smile, a frown, an open hand, a clenched fist, an erect spine or bowed shoulders, respectively. We also know that certain feelings will cause the eye to sparkle or grow dim, the voice to become resonant and positive or to become husky and weak; according to the nature of the feelings.

Prof. Wm. James says: "What kind of emotion of fear would be left if the feeling neither of trembling lips nor of weakened limbs, neither of goose-flesh nor of visceral stirrings, were present, it is quite impossible for me to think. Can one fancy the state of rage and picture no ebullition in the chest, no flushing of the face, no dilation of the nostrils, no clenching of the teeth, no impulse to vigorous action, but in their stead limp muscles, calm breathing, and a placid face?"

Prof. Halleck says: "All the emotions have well-defined muscular expression. Darwin has written an excellent work entitled, *The Expression of the Emotions in Man and Animals,* to which students must refer for a detailed account of such expression. A very few examples must suffice here. In all the exhilarating emotions, the eyebrows, the eyelids, the nostrils, and the angles of the mouth are raised. In the depressing passions it is the reverse. This general statement conveys so much truth, that a careful observer can read a large part of the history of a human being written in the face. For this reason many phrenologists have wisely turned physiognomists. Grief is expressed by raising the inner ends of the eyebrows, drawing down the corners of the mouth, and transversely wrinkling the middle part of the forehead. In Terra del Fuego, a party of natives conveyed to Darwin the idea that a certain man was low-spirited, by pulling down their cheeks in order to make their faces long. Joy is expressed by drawing backward and upward the corners of the mouth. The upper lip rises and draws the cheeks upward, forming wrinkles under the eyes. The elevation of the upper lip and the nostrils expresses contempt. A skillful observer can frequently tell if one person admires another. In this case the eyebrows are raised, disclosing a brightening eye and a relaxed expression; sometimes a gentle smile plays about the mouth. Blushing is merely the physical expression of certain emotions. We notice the expression of emotion more in the countenance, because the effects are there more plainly visible; but the muscles of the entire body, the vital organs, and the viscera, are also vehicles of expression."

These things need but a mention in order to be recognized and admitted. This is the *action* of the Inner upon the Outer. There is, however, a *reaction* of the Outer upon the Inner, which while equally true is not so generally recognized nor admitted, and we think it well to briefly call your attention to the same, for the reason that this correspondence between the Inner and the Outer—this *reaction* as well as the *action*—must be appreciated in order that the entire meaning and content of the subject of Human Nature may be fully grasped.

That the *reaction* of the Outer Form upon the Inner State may be understood, we ask you to consider the following opinions of well-known and accepted authorities of the New Psychology, regarding the established fact that a *physical expression related to a mental state, will, if voluntarily induced, tend to in turn induce the mental state appropriate to it.* We have used these quotations in other books of this series, but will insert them here in this place because they have a direct bearing upon the particular subject before us, and because they furnish direct and unquestioned authority for the statements just made by us. We ask you to consider them carefully, for they express a most important truth.

Prof. Halleck says: "By inducing an expression we can often cause its allied emotion. . . . Actors have frequently testified to the fact that emotion will arise if they go through the appropriate muscular movements. In talking to a character on the stage, if they clench the fist and frown, they often find themselves becoming really angry; if they start with counterfeit laughter, they find themselves growing cheerful. A German professor says that he cannot walk with a schoolgirl's mincing step and air without feeling frivolous."

Prof. Wm. James says: "Whistling to keep up courage is no mere figure of speech.

On the other hand, sit all day in a moping posture, sigh, and reply to everything with a dismal voice, and your melancholy lingers. If we wish to conquer undesirable emotional tendencies in ourselves, we must assiduously, and in the first instance coldbloodedly, go through the *outward movements* of those contrary dispositions which we wish to cultivate. Smooth the brow, brighten the eye, contract the dorsal rather than the ventral aspect of the frame, and speak in a major key, pass the genial compliment, and your heart must indeed be frigid if it does not gradually thaw."

Dr. Wood Hutchinson, says: "To what extent muscular contractions condition emotions, as Prof. James has suggested, may be easily tested by a quaint and simple little experiment upon a group of the smallest voluntary muscles of the body, those that move the eyeball. Choose some time when you are sitting quietly in your room, free from all disturbing influences. Then stand up, and assuming an easy position, cast the eyes upward and hold them in that position for thirty seconds. Instantly and involuntarily you will be conscious of a tendency toward reverential, devotional, contemplative ideas and thoughts. Then turn the eyes sideways, glancing directly to the right or to the left, through half-closed lids. Within thirty seconds images of suspicion, of uneasiness, or of dislike will rise unbidden to the mind. Turn the eyes on one side and slightly downward, and suggestions of jealousy or coquetry will be apt to spring unbidden. Direct your gaze downward toward the floor, and you are likely to go off into a fit of reverie or abstraction."

Prof. Maudsley says: "The specific muscular action is not merely an exponent of passion, but truly an essential part of it. If we try while the features are fixed in the expression of one passion to call up in the mind a different one, we shall find it impossible to do so."

We state the fact of the *reaction* of the Outer upon the Inner, with its supporting quotations from the authorities, not for the purpose of instructing our readers in the art of training the emotions by means of the physical, for while this subject is highly important, it forms no part of the particular subject under our present consideration—but that the student may realize the close relationship existing between the Inner State and the Outer Form. These two elements or phases, in their constant action and reaction, manifest the phenomena of Human Nature, and a knowledge of each, and both give to us the key which will open for us the door of the understanding of Human Nature.

Let us now call your attention to an illustration which embodies both principles—that of the Inner and the Outer—and the action and reaction between them, as given by that master of subtle ratiocination, Edgar Allan Poe. Poe in his story "The Purloined Letter" tells of a boy at school who attained great proficiency in the game of "even or odd" in which one player strives to guess whether the marbles held in the hand of his opponent are odd or even. The boy's plan was to gauge the intelligence of his opponent regarding the matter of making changes, and as Poe says: "this lay in mere observation and admeasurement of the astuteness of his opponents." Poe describes the process as follows: "For example, an arrant simpleton is his opponent, and, holding up his closed hand, asks, 'are they even or odd?' Our schoolboy replies, 'odd,' and loses; but upon the second trial he wins, for he then says to himself, 'the simpleton had them even upon the first trial, and his amount of cunning is just sufficient to make him have them odd upon the second; I will therefore guess odd;' —he guesses and wins. Now, with a simpleton a degree above the first, he would have reasoned thus: 'This fellow finds that in the first instance I guessed odd, and, in the second, he will propose to himself upon the first impulse, a simple variation from even to odd, as did the first simpleton; but then a second thought will suggest that this is too simple a variation, and finally he will decide upon putting it even as before. I will therefore guess even;' he guesses even and wins."

Poe continues by stating that this "is merely an identification of the reasoner's intellect with that of his opponent. Upon inquiring of the boy by what means he effected the *thorough* identification in which his success consisted, I received answer as follows: 'When I wish to find out how wise, or how stupid, or how good, or how wicked is any one, or what are his thoughts at the moment, *I fashion the expression of my face, as accurately as possible in accordance with the expression of his, and then wait to see what thoughts or sentiments arise in my mind or heart, as if to match or correspond with the expression.'* This response of the school boy lies at the bottom of all the spurious profundity which has been attributed to Rochefoucauld, to La Bougive, to Machiavelli, and to Campanella."

In this consideration of Human Nature we shall have much to say about the Outer Form. But we must ask the reader to always remember that the Outer Form is always the expression and manifestation of the Inner State, be that Inner State latent and dormant within the depths of the subconscious mentality, or else active and dynamic in conscious expression. Just as Prof. James so strongly insists, we cannot imagine an inner feeling or emotion without its corresponding outward physical expression, so is it impossible to imagine the outward expressions generally associated with a particular feeling or emotion without its corresponding inner state. Whether or not one of these, the outer or inner, is the *cause* of the other—and if so, *which one* is the cause and which the effect—need not concern us here. In fact, it would seem more reasonable to accept the theory that they are correlated and appear simultaneously. Many careful thinkers have held that action and reaction are practically the same thing—merely the opposite phases of the same fact. If this be so, then indeed when we are studying the Outer Form of Human Nature we are studying psychology just as much as when we are studying the Inner States. Prof. Wm. James in his works upon psychology insists upon the relevancy of the consideration of the outward expressions of the inner feeling and emotion, as we have seen. The same authority speaks even more emphatically upon this phase of the subject, as follows:

"The feeling, in the coarser emotions, results from the bodily expression. . . . My theory is that the bodily changes follow directly the perception of the exciting fact, and that our feeling of the same changes as they occur *is* the emotion. . . . Particular perceptions certainly do produce widespread bodily effects by a sort of immediate physical influence, antecedent to the arousal of an emotion or emotional idea. . . . Every one of the bodily changes, whatsoever it may be, is *felt*, acutely or obscurely, the moment it occurs. . . . If we fancy some strong emotion, and then try to abstract from our consciousness of it all the feelings of its bodily symptoms, we have nothing left behind. . . . A disembodied human emotion is a sheer nonentity. I do not say that it is a contradiction in the nature of things, or that pure spirits are necessarily condemned to cold intellectual lives; but I say that for *us* emotion disassociated from all bodily feeling is inconceivable. The more closely I scrutinize my states, the more persuaded I become that whatever 'coarse' affections and passions I have are in very truth constituted by, and made up of, those bodily changes which we ordinarily call their expression or consequence. . . . But our emotions must always be *inwardly* what they are, whatever may be the physiological ground of their apparition. If they are deep, pure, worthy, spiritual facts on any conceivable theory of their physiological source, they remain no less deep, pure, spiritual, and worthy of regard on this present sensational theory."

Kay says: "Does the mind or spirit of man, whatever it may be, in its actings in and through the body, leave a material impression or trace in its structure of every conscious action it performs, which remains permanently fixed, and forms a material record of all that it has done in the body, to which it can afterward refer as to a book and recall to mind, making it again, as it were, present to it? . . . We find nature everywhere around us recording its movements and marking the changes it has undergone in material forms,—in the crust of the earth, the composition of the rocks, the structure of the trees, the conformation of our bodies, and those spirits of ours, so closely connected with our material bodies, that so far as we know, they can think no thought, perform no action, without their presence and co-operation, may have been so joined in order to preserve a material and lasting record of all that they think and do."

Marsh says: "Every human movement, every organic act, every volition, passion, or emotion, every intellectual process, is accompanied with atomic disturbance." Picton says: "The soul never does one single action by itself apart from some excitement of bodily tissue." Emerson says: "The rolling rock leaves its scratches on the mountain; the river its channel in the soil; the animal its bones in the stratum; the fern and leaf their modest epitaph in the coal. The falling drop makes its sculpture in the sand or stone. . . . The ground is all memoranda and signatures, and every object covered over with hints which speak to the intelligent. In nature this self-registration is incessant." Morell says: "The mind depends for the manifestation of all its activities upon a material organism." Bain says: "The organ of the mind is not the brain by itself; it is the brain, nerve, muscles, organs of sense, viscera. . . . It is uncertain how far even thought, reminiscence, or the emotions of the past and absent could be sustained without the more distant communication between the brain and the rest of the body." And, thus, as we consider the subject carefully we see that psychology is as much concerned with the physical manifestations of the mental impulses and states as with the metaphysical aspect of those states—as much with the Outer Form as with the Inner State—for it is practically impossible to permanently separate them.

As an illustration of the physical accompaniment or Outer Form, of the psychical feeling or Inner State, the following quotation from Darwin's "Origin of the Emotions," will well serve the purpose:

"Fear is often preceded by astonishment, and is so far akin to it that both lead to the senses of sight and hearing being instantly aroused. In both cases the eyes and mouth are widely opened and the eyebrows raised. The frightened man at first stands like a statue, motionless and breathless, or crouches down as if instinctively to escape observation. The heart beats quickly and violently, so that it palpitates or knocks against the ribs; but it is very doubtful if it then works more efficiently than usual, so as to send a greater supply of blood to all parts of the body; for the skin instantly becomes pale as during incipient faintness. This paleness of the surface, however, is probably in large part, or is exclusively, due to the vaso-motor centre being affected in such a manner as to cause the contraction of the small arteries of the skin. That the skin is much affected under the sense of great fear, we see in the marvelous manner in which perspiration immediately exudes from it. This exudation is all the more remarkable, as the surface is then cold, and hence the term, a cold sweat; whereas the sudorific glands are properly excited into action when the surface is heated. The hairs also on the skin stand erect, and the superficial muscles shiver. In connection with the disturbed action of the heart the breathing is hurried. The salivary glands act imperfectly; the mouth becomes dry and is often opened and shut. I have noticed that under slight fear there is a strong tendency to yawn. One of the best marked symptoms is the trembling of all the muscles of the body; and this is often seen in the lips.

From this cause, and from the dryness of the mouth, the voice becomes husky or indistinct or may altogether fail. . . . As fear increases into an agony of terror, we behold, as under all violent emotions, diversified results. The heart beats wildly or fails to act and faintness ensues; there is a death-like pallor; the breathing is labored; the wings of the nostrils are widely dilated; there is a gasping and convulsive motion of the lips; a tremor of the hollow cheek, a gulping and catching of the throat; the uncovered and protruding eyeballs are fixed on the object of terror; or they may roll restlessly from side to side. The pupils are said to be enormously dilated. All the muscles of the body may become rigid or may be thrown into convulsive movements. The hands are alternately clenched and opened, often with a twitching movement. The arms may be protruded as if to avert some dreadful danger, or may be thrown wildly over the head. The Rev. Mr. Hagenauer has seen this latter action in a terrified Australian. In other cases there is a sudden and uncontrolled tendency to headlong flight; and so strong is this that the boldest soldiers may be seized with a sudden panic."

In conclusion, let us say that just as the above striking description of the master-scientist, Darwin, shows us that the particular emotion has its outer manifestations—the particular Inner State its Outer Form—so has the general *character* of the person its outer manifestation, and Outer Form. And, just as to the eye of the experienced observer at a distance (even in the case of a photographic representation, particularly in the case of a moving picture) may recognize the Inner State from the Outer Form of the feeling or emotion, so may the experienced character reader interpret the whole character of the person from the Outer Form thereof. The two interpretations are based on exactly the same general principles. The inner thought and feeling manifest in the outer physical form. He who learns the alphabet of Outer Form may read page after page of the book of Human Nature.

CHAPTER II

THE INNER PHASE: CHARACTER

Do you know what "character" is? The word itself, in its derivation and original usage, means: "a stamp, mark or sign, engraved or stamped." As time passed the term was applied to the personal peculiarities of individuals, and was defined as: "the personal qualities or attributes of a person; the distinguishing traits of a person. Later the term was extended to mean: "the part enacted by anyone in a play." In the common usage of the term we seek to convey an idea in which each and all of the above stated meanings are combined. A man's character is the result of *impressions* made upon his own mind, or those of the race. It is also the sum of his personal qualities and attributes. It is also, in a sense, the part he plays in the great drama of life.

Each man's character has its inner phase consisting of the accumulated impressions of the past which seek to manifest in the present. And, likewise, the character of each man manifests in an outer phase of form, mark, and stamp of *personality.* There are no two characters precisely alike. There is an infinite possibility of combination of the elements that go to make up character. This is accordance with what appears to be a universal law of nature, for there are no two blades of grass exactly alike, nor two grains of sand bearing an exact resemblance to each other. Nature seems to seek after and to manifest variety of form and quality. But, still, just as we may classify all things, animate and inanimate, into general classes and then into subordinate ones—each genus and each species having its particular characteristics, qualities and attributes, so we may, and do, classify human character into general classes and then into particular subdivisions into which each individual is found to fit. This fact makes it possible for us to study Human Nature as a science.

The character of each individual is held to be the result of the impressions made upon the plastic material of the mind, either in the form of past impressions upon his ancestors or of past impressions received by the individual. The past impressions reach him through the channel of heredity, while the personal impressions come to him through environment. But by heredity we do not mean the transmission of the personal characteristics of one's parents or even grandparents, but something far deeper and broader. We believe that one inherits far less of the qualities of one's parents than is generally believed. But, we believe that much that goes to make up our character is derived from the associated qualities and impressions of many generations of ancestors. Inasmuch as each individual contains within him the transmitted qualities of nearly every individual who lived several thousand years ago, it may be said that each individual is an heir to the accumulated impressions of the race, which however form in an infinite variety of combinations, the result being that although the root of the race is the same yet each individual differs in combination from each other individual. As Luther Burbank has said: "Heredity means much, but what is heredity? Not some hideous ancestral specter, forever crossing the path of a human being. Heredity is simply the sum of all the effects of all the environments of all past generations on the responsive ever-moving life-forces."

The records of the past environment of the race are stored away in the great region of the subconscious mentality, from whence they arise in response to the call of some attractive object of thought or perception, always, however, modified and restrained by the opposite characteristics. As Prof. Elmer Gates has said: "At least ninety per cent of our mental life is sub-conscious. If you will analyze your mental operations you will find that conscious thinking is never a continuous line of consciousness, but a series of conscious data with great intervals of subconsciousness. We sit and try to solve a problem and fail. We walk around, try again and fail. Suddenly an idea dawns that leads to a solution of the problem. The sub-conscious processes were at work. We do not volitionally create our own thinking. It takes place in us. We are more or less passive recipients. We cannot change the nature of a thought, or of a truth, but we can, as it were, guide the ship by a moving of the helm."

But character is dependent upon race inheritance only for its raw materials, which are then worked into shape by the influence of environment and by the will of the individual. A man's environment is, to some extent at least, dependent upon the will. A man may change his environment, and by the use of his will he may overcome many inherited tendencies. As Halleck well says: "Heredity is a powerful factor, for it supplies raw material for the will to shape. Even the will cannot make anything without material. Will acts through choice, and some kinds of environment afford far more opportunities for choice than others. Shakespeare found in London the germ of true theatrical taste, already vivified by a long line of miracle plays, moralities and interludes. In youth he connected himself with the theatre, and his will responded powerfully to his environment. Some surroundings are rich in suggestion, affording opportunity for choice, while others are poor. The will is absolutely confined to a choice between alternatives. *Character then, is a resultant of will power, heredity and environment.* The modern tendency is to overestimate the effects of heredity and environment in forming character; but, on the other hand, we must not underestimate them. The child of a Hottentot put in Shakespeare's home, and afterward sent away to London with him, would never have made a Shakespeare; for heredity would not have given the will sufficient raw material to fashion over into such a noble product. We may also suppose a case to show the great power of environment. Had a band of gypsies stolen Shakespeare at birth, carried him to Tartary, and left him among the nomads, his environment would never have allowed him to produce such plays as he placed upon the English stage."

Many persons are reluctant to admit the effect of heredity upon character. They seem to regard heredity as the idea of a monster ruling the individual with an iron hand, and with an emphasis upon undesirable traits of character. Such people lose sight of the fact that at the best heredity merely supplies us with the raw material of character rather than the finished product, and that *there is much good in this raw material.* We receive our inheritance of good as well as bad. Deprive a man of the advantage of his heredity, and we place him back to the plane of the savage, or perhaps still lower in the scale. Heredity is simply the shoulders of the race affording us a place for our feet, in order that we may rise higher than those who lived before. For *heredity,* substitute *evolution,* and we may get a clearer idea of this element of character.

As for environment, it is folly to deny its influence. Take two young persons of equal ability, similar tastes, and the same heredity, and place them one in a small village, and the other in a great metropolis, and keep them there until middle-age, and we will see the influence of environment. The two may be equally happy and contented, and may possess the same degree of book-education, but, nevertheless, their experiences will have been so different that the character of the two individuals must be different. In the same way, place the two young persons, one in the Whitechapel district, and the other amidst the best surroundings and example, and see the result. Remember, that in *environment* is included the influence of other persons. The effect of environment arises from Suggestion, that great moulding and creative principle of the mind. It is true that, "As a man thinketh, so is he," but a man's thoughts depend materially upon the *associations* of environment, experience, and suggestion. As Ziehen says: "We cannot think as we will, but we must think as just those associations which happen to be present prescribe."

But, without going further into the question of the elements which go toward forming character, let us take our position firmly upon the fact that each individual is stamped with the impression of a special character—a character all his own. Each has his own *character* or part to play in the great drama of life. The character of some seems fixed and unchangeable, while that of others is seen to be in the process of change. But in either case each and every man has his own character or manifestation of Human Nature, in its inner and outer aspects. And each individual, while in a sense forming a special class by himself, nevertheless belongs to a larger class, which in turn is a part of a still larger, and so on.

Instead of studying the philosophy or metaphysics of character, or even its general psychology, let us in this particular volume devote our attention to the elements which go to form the character of each and every person, so that we may understand them when we meet them in manifested form. And let us learn the Outer Form which accompany these Inner States.

Upon the stage of Life move backward and forward many characters, each having his or her own form, manner and appearance, which like those of the characters upon the mimic stage, may be recognized if we will but bestow a little care upon the subject. The Othellos, Hamlets, Shylocks, Iagos, Richards, Lears, and the rest are to be found in every-day life. The Micawbers, Chuzzlewits, Twists, and the rest are in as full evidence on the streets and in the offices, as in the books. The person who is able to read and interpret Human Nature is possessed of a knowledge far more useful to him than that contained within the covers of musty books upon impractical subjects.

CHAPTER III

THE OUTER PHASE: PERSONALITY

Just as *character* is the inner phase of Human Nature, so is *personality* its outer phase. To many the two terms are synonymous, but analysis will show the shades of difference between them. A man's *character* is his inner self, while his *personality* is the outward indication of his self. The word, in this sense, is defined as: "That which constitutes the personal traits of a person, as his manner, conduct, habits, appearance, and other observable personal peculiarities."

The word is derived from the Latin word, *persona,* meaning, "a mask used by play-actors," which in turn was derived from the two words *per*, meaning "through," and *sono,* meaning, "to sound," or combined, "to sound through." And the derivation of the term really gives us an idea of its inner meaning, for the personality is really the mask worn by the character, and *through which it sounds,* speaks, or manifests itself, Jeremy Taylor once said: "No man can long put on *person* and act a part but his evil manners will peep through the corners of his white robe." Archbishop Trench once said that the real meaning of the phrase, "God is no respecter of *persons*" is that the Almighty cared nothing for what *part* in life a person plays, but *how* he plays it. The old-time play-actor was wont to assume a mask of the features of the part he played, just as the modern actor "makes up" for the part and walks, speaks and acts in accordance therewith. Whether or not the individual be aware of the fact, Nature furnishes to each his mask of personality—his *persona*—by which those who understand may recognize the part he plays, or his character. In both the inner *character*, and the outer *personality*, each individual struts the stage of life and plays his part.

The mask or "make up," of personality, by which men may read each other's character, is evolved and developed from the instinctive physical expression accompanying thought, feeling and emotion. Just as the frown accompanying the feeling of annoyance or anger will, if repeated sufficiently often, become fixed upon the countenance of the man, so will all of his general thoughts, feelings and emotions register themselves in his manner, gait, tone of voice, carriage and facial expression. Moreover, his inherited tendencies will show themselves in the same way.

Professor Wm. James says, regarding the genesis of emotional reactions: "How come the various objects which excite emotion to produce such special and different bodily effects? This question was not asked till quite recently, but already some interesting suggestions toward answering it have been made. Some movements of expression can be accounted for as weakened repetitions of movements which formerly (when they were stronger) were of utility to the subject. Others are similarly weakened repetitions of movements which under other conditions were physiologically necessary concomitants of the useful movements. Of the latter reactions, the respiratory disturbances in anger and fear might be taken as examples—organic reminiscences, as it were, reverberations in imagination of the blowings of the man making a series of combative efforts, or the pantings of one in precipitate flight. Such at least is a suggestion made by Mr. Spencer which has found approval.''

Herbert Spencer says, on this subject: To have in a slight degree such psychical states as accompany the reception of wounds, and are experienced during flight, is to be in a state of what we call fear. And to have in a slight degree such psychical states as the processes of catching, killing, and eating imply, is to have the desires to catch, kill and eat. That the propensities to the acts are nothing else than nascent excitations of the psychical state involved in the acts, is proved by the natural language of the propensities. Fear, when strong, expresses itself in cries, in efforts to escape in palpitations, in tremblings; and these are just the manifestations that go along with an actual suffering of the evil feared. The destructive passion is shown in a general tension of the muscular system, in gnashing of teeth and protrusion of the claws, in dilated eyes and nostrils in growls; and these are weaker forms of the actions that accompany the killing of prey. To such objective evidences every one can add subjective evidences. Everyone can testify that the psychical state called fear consists of mental representations of certain painful results; and that the one called anger consists of mental representations of the actions and impressions which would occur while inflicting some kind of pain."

Professor Wm. James adds the following to the discussion: "So slight a symptom as the snarl or sneer, the one-sided uncovering of the upper teeth, is accounted for by Darwin as a survival from the time when our ancestors had large canines, and unfleshed him (as dogs do now) for attack. Similarly the raising of the eyebrows in outward attention, the opening of the mouth in astonishment, come, according to the same author, from the utility of these movements in extreme cases. The raising of the eyebrows goes with the opening of the eye for better vision, the opening of the mouth with the intensest listening, and with the rapid catching of the breath which precedes muscular effort. The distension of the nostrils in anger is interpreted by Spencer as an echo of the way in which our ancestors had to breathe when, during combat, their 'mouth was filled up by a part of an antagonists's body that had been seized.' The trembling of fear is supposed by Mantegazza to be for the sake of warming the blood. The reddening of the face and neck is called by Wundt a compensatory arrangement for relieving the brain of the blood-pressure which the simultaneous excitement of the heart brings with it. The effusion of tears is explained both by this author and by Darwin to be a blood-withdrawing agency of a similar sort. The contraction of the muscles around the eyes, of which the primitive use is to protect those organs from being too much gorged with blood during the screaming fits of infancy, survives in adult life in the shape of the frown, which instantly comes over the brow when anything difficult or displeasing presents itself either to thought or action."

Thus, it will be seen, the fact that all inward states manifest themselves to some degree in outward physical expression, brings with it the logical inference that particular mental states when habitually manifested tend to fix in the physical organism the expression associated with them. As "thoughts take form in action," so habitual mental states tend to register traces of those actions. A piece of paper folded in a certain way several times shows plainly the marks on the folding. In the same manner the creases in our clothing, shoes and gloves, show the marks of our personal physical form. A habitual mental state of cheerfulness is accompanied by a frequent exercise of the muscles expressing the physical signs of that feeling, and finally the smile wrinkles are formed that all may read them. In the same way the gloomy, pessimistic mental attitude produces the marks and wrinkles showing the habit of frequent down-turning of the corners of our mouths. A habitual mental attitude of suspicion will tend to impart the appearance of the "suspicious peering" to our eyes. The mental attitude of combativeness will likewise give us the traditional set jaw and tightly compressed lips. The mental attitude of lack of self-respect will show itself in our walk, and so, in the opposite manner with the mental attitude of self-respect. People grow to walk, talk, carry themselves, and "look like" their habitual mental attitude.

Dr. A. T. Schofield, says: "'He is a dull scholar,' it is said, 'who cannot read a man's character even from a back view.' Round a statue of the prince Consort in Edinburgh stand representative groups paying homage to him. If you get a back view of any of these you can see unconscious mind impressed on matter, and can tell at once the sailor or soldier, peasant or scholar or workman. Look at the body and face of a man when the mind is gone. Look at the body of a man who has lost his self-respect. Look at the body of a thief, of a sot, of a miser. Compare the faces and expressions of a philanthropist, of a beggar, of a policeman, of a scholar, of a sailor, of a lawyer, of a doctor, of a shop-walker, of a sandwich man, of a farmer, of a successful manufacturer, of a nurse, of a refined girl, of a servant, of a barmaid, of a nun, of a ballet dancer, of an art student, and answer to yourself these two questions: First, are these different expressions of body and face due essentially to *physical* or *psychical* causes? And, secondly, do these psychical causes act on the facial and other muscles in consciousness or out of consciousness. The only possible answers to these two questions leave us with this fact, were no other proof possible, that we each have within us an unconscious *psychical* power (here called the unconscious mind) which has sufficient force to act upon the body and display psychical conceptions through physical media."

It is impossible for us (at least by any of the five senses) to peer into the mental chamber of other men and there read the record of their *character,* or to interpret the combination of Human Nature therein moulded and formed. But nevertheless we are not balked in our desire, for by learning to interpret the outward signs of personality we may arrive with a wonderful degree of success at an understanding of the character, mind, or Human Nature in others. From the seen Outer we may deduce the unseen Inner. We may discern the shape of that which is concealed, by observing the form of the covering which hides it from sight. The body, like the fabled veil of the goddess, "conceals but to reveal."

CHAPTER IV

THE TEMPERAMENTS

The student of Human Nature soon discovers that among men, as among the animals, there is to be observed a great variety of "quality," and various classes of "temperament." Among cattle we notice great differences of form which differences indicate certain qualities inherent in the beast. Certain qualities are recognized by their outward forms as being indicative of sturdiness, staying-qualities, strong vitality, etc., which render their possessor valuable for draught oxen. Other qualities indicate the value of another animal for meat producing. Others, the production of large quantities of milk. Others, prolific breeding. And, so on, each set of qualities being recognized by its outward form and being taken into consideration by breeders. In the same way, breeders recognize certain qualities in horses which they take advantage of in breeding for the strength of draught horses; the speed of thoroughbred runners and trotters; the docility and gentleness of driving horses and saddle animals. The draught horse and the thoroughbred runner or trotter may be easily distinguished by the eye of the average person, while it requires the eye of the expert to distinguish other points and signs of quality which prove the existence of certain traits of temperament in the animal. The same is true in the case of chickens and other fowls. Some types are adapted for laying, others for meat purposes, others for gameness, etc. Not only the physical qualities but also the temperamental traits of the beast or bird are distinguished by the expert, and are taken advantage of in breeding to develop and evolve the indicated trait or quality.

Nearly anyone may distinguish the temperamental difference between the savage dog and the affectionate one—between the vicious horse and the docile one. We know at once that certain dogs may be approached and others kept at a distance—that certain horses are safe to ride or drive, and that others are unsafe and dangerous. A visit to a horse and cattle show, or a poultry and pigeon exhibition, will show even the most skeptical person that Inner States manifest in Outer Form. And a little further study and observation will show that what is true of these lower animals is likewise true of the human being. Men, like animals, may be intelligently and scientifically classified according to the general "quality" or "temperament." While each individual is different in a way from every other individual, nevertheless, each individual belongs to a certain class and may be labelled accordingly. A few outward signs will indicate his class, and we may confidently expect that he will manifest the leading qualities of that particular class.

QUALITY

The first classification of the individuals of the human race is that of *Quality*. Independent of the various temperaments, although in a way related to them, we find the various degrees of Quality manifested by different individuals. "Quality" may be defined as the "degree of *fineness*." It is that which we call "class" in race-horses; "breed" in other animals and often "blood" in men and women. Perhaps one may understand the classification better if he will recall the differences apparent between the mongrel cur and the highbred dog; the "scrub" horse and the thoroughbred; the common cow and the carefully bred Alderney or other choice variety; the ordinary barnyard fowl and the prize-winner at the poultry show. It is an intangible but real and readily recognized difference, which however is almost impossible to convey by words.

Men and women of the highest *Quality* are essentially fine-grained, possessed of fine feelings, refined natures, high tastes, and manifest the signs of *true natural* refinement and culture, which cannot be successfully imitated by those who have acquired merely the artificial manner and the outward polish. One may possess Quality in a high degree and still be ignorant of the forms and little manners of so-called "polite society," and yet will be recognized as one of "Nature's noblemen," and as a "natural gentleman."

Descending the scale we find lessening degrees of the manifestation of Quality, until, finally we reach the lowest degree of the scale, that of *low* Quality. In this lowest degree we find individuals showing all the outward signs of being coarse-grained, vulgar, of low tastes, brutal instincts, and manifesting the signs of lack of refinement and culture. Persons of low Quality are found in all walks of life. Some of those possessing wealth and education belong to this class, and are never able to counterfeit the reality. Quality is a matter of "soul," and not of wealth, education or material advantages. A greyhound and a hyena give us animal symbols of Quality, high and low.

We meet many instances in which the individual is of too high Quality for his environment, occupation or place in life. Such individuals suffer keenly and are to be pitied. They incline toward high ideals and are wounded and discouraged by the grossness which they see on all sides. Those individuals of an average degree of Quality of course fit into the usual environment far better than those above or below them in the scale. We also meet individuals of low Quality in surroundings in which they are out of place—we see many instances of "pigs in the parlor.'' These individuals, however, find it much easier to descend to their own level, than it is for the high Quality individuals to ascend to theirs. The coarse man finds but little trouble in meeting with boon companions whose tastes are harmonious to his. The person of extremely high Quality may be said to have been born before his time, while those of the lowest Quality are atavistic and born after their time. Remember, always, that Quality is an attribute of ''soul,'' and not of birth, wealth, or even of education. We may find many ''gentlemen'' of humble birth, small means and limited education; and also many ''educated pigs'' of high lineage and full coffers.

The Outer Form of Quality is shown by the relative *fineness* of general structure, and by the general form, appearance, manner, motion, voice, laughter, and more than all by that indescribable impression of ''fineness'' and ''distinction'' which they produce upon observing persons with whom they come in contact.

It must be remembered that Quality is a very different thing from intellectuality or morality. A high Quality person may be immoral and not specially intellectual, although there is almost always a *keenness* of perception, and almost intuitive recognition, in these cases—the immorality is generally lacking in coarseness, and is usually connected with perversion of the æsthetic faculties. In the same way, the person of low Quality often may be moral according to the code, but will be coarse in the manifestation of that virtue, and may possess a certain low cunning which with many persons passes for intellect and "brains." In speaking of Quality, the words "fineness" and "coarseness" come easily to the mind and tongue and are perhaps the terms most suggestive of the two extremes of this attribute of the Man.

TEMPERAMENT

Next in the order of consideration we find what is called *Temperament*. Temperament is defined as: "That individual peculiarity of organization by which the manner of acting, feeling and thinking of each person is permanently affected; disposition or constitution of the mind, especially as regards the passions and affections.''

Hippocrates, the ancient Greek philosopher-physician (B. C. 468—367) held to the existence of four temperaments, which he attributed to certain qualities of the blood and the several secretions of the body such as the bile, etc. While his theory was rejected by later investigators, his classification continued until very recently under the name of (1) the Sanguine; (2) the Lymphatic or Phlegmatic; (3) the Choleric or Bilious; and (4) the Melancholic temperaments, respectively. As a matter of general information on the subject we herewith give the old classification with the attributes of each class:

The *Sanguine* temperament was held to be characterized by red or light-brown hair, blue eyes, a fair or ruddy complexion, large arteries and veins, a full and rapid pulse, slight perspiration, impatience of heat, febrile tendency, and lively and cheerful temper, excitable passions, a warm, ardent, impulsive disposition, and a liking for active pursuits;

The *Lymphatic*, or *Phlegmatic* temperament was held to be characterized by light, sandy, or whitish hair, light grey eyes, pallid complexion, skin almost devoid of hair, flabby tissues, much perspiration, small blood-vessels, a feeble and slow pulse, want of energy, lack of activity, deficient spirit and vividness;

The *Choleric* or *Bilious* temperament was held to be characterized by black hair often curling, black or hazel eyes, and dark but ruddy complexion, hairy skin, strong full pulse, firm muscles, great activity and positiveness, strength of character, and an active brain.

The *Melancholic* temperament was held to be characterized by black hair, black or hazel eyes, a dark leaden complexion, pulse slow and feeble, and a disposition toward study, poetry, literature, and sentiment.

Some later authorities added a fifth temperament, called the *Nervous* temperament, which was held to be characterized by a medium complexion, large brain, small physical frame, fineness of organization, thin hair, finely cut features, quick lively disposition, intellectual tastes and tendencies, sensitive nature, high capacity for enjoyment and suffering.

The latest authorities, however, discarded the old classification and adopted one more simple although fully as comprehensive. The new classification recognizes *three* classes of temperament, viz: (1) the Vital; (2) the Motive; and (3) the Mental, the characteristics of which are held to be as follows:

The *Vital* temperament has its basis in the predominance of the nutritive system, including the blood-vessels, lymphatics and the glands. Its organs are the heart, lungs, stomach, liver, bowels, and the entire internal vital system. It is characterized by a large, broad frame; broad shoulders; deep chest; full round abdomen; round plump limbs; short thick neck; comparatively small hands and feet; full face; flushed and florid cheeks; and general "well fed" appearance. Those in whom it is predominant are fond of out-of-door exercise, although not of hard work; crave the "good things of life;" fond of sport, games and play; love variety of entertainment and amusement; are affectionate; love praise and flattery; prefer concrete rather than abstract subjects of thought; look out for themselves; are selfish, but yet "good fellows" when it does not cost too much physical discomfort to themselves; usually enjoy good health, yet when ill are apt to be very weak; tend to feverishness and apoplexy, etc.

Persons of the Vital temperament may have either fair or dark complexion, but in either case the cheeks and face are apt to be ruddy and flushed. Those of the dark type are apt to have greater power of endurance, while those of the light type are apt to be more sprightly and active. This temperament is particularly noticeable in women, a large proportion of whom belong to its class. This temperament furnishes the majority of the good companions, sociable friends and acquaintances, and theatre goers. A leading phrenologist says of them that they "incline to become agents, overseers, captains, hotel-keepers, butchers, traders, speculators, politicians, public officers, aldermen, contractors, etc., rather than anything requiring steady or hard work." We have noticed that a large number of railroad engineers and policemen are of this temperament.

The *Motive* temperament has as its basis the predominance of the motive or mechanical system, including the muscles, bones and ligaments—the general system of active work and motion. Its organs are those of the entire framework of the body, together with those muscles and ligaments, large and small, general and special, which enable man to walk, move, and work. It is characterized by strong constitution, physical power, strong character, active feeling, and tendency toward work; large bones and joints; hard muscles; angular and rugged figure; usually broad shoulders and deep chest; comparatively small and flat abdomen; oblong face; large jaw; high cheek-bones; strong large teeth; bushy coarse hair; rugged features and prominent nose, ears, mouth, etc. Those in whom it is predominant are fond of physical and mental work; are tenacious and try to carry through what they undertake; resist fatigue; are "good stayers;" are full of dogged persistence and resistance; and are apt to manifest creative effort and work.

Persons of the Motive temperament may have either dark or light complexion. The Scotch or Scandanavian people show this temperament strongly, as also do a certain type of Americans. The world's active workers come chiefly from this class. This temperament is far more common among men than among women. The fighting nations who have in different times swept over other countries display this temperament strongly. This temperament, predominant, although associated with the other temperaments has distinguished the "men who do things" in the world's history. It's "rawbone" and gawkiness has swept things before it, and has built up great things in all times. Its individuals have a burning desire to "take hold and pull," or to "get together and start something." As the name implies, this temperament is the "moving force" in mankind.

The *Mental* temperament has its basis in the predominance of the nervous system, including the brain and spinal cord. Its organs are the brain, or brains; the spinal cord with its connecting nerves—in fact the entire nervous system, including the "sympathetic" nervous system, the various *plexi*, and the nervous substance found in various parts of the body. It is characterized by a light build; slight frame; comparatively large head; quick movements; sharp features; thin sharp nose; thin lips; sharp and not very strong teeth; keen, penetrating eye; high forehead and upper head; fondness for brain work; disinclination for physical drudgery; sensitive nature; quick perception; rapid mental action; developed intuition; fine and shapely features; expressive countenance, expressive and striking voice, generally rather "high-strung," vividness and intensity of emotion and feeling, etc.

Persons of this temperament are apt to be more or less "intense;" enjoy and suffer keenly; are sensitive to reproach or criticism; are inclined to be sedentary; take a pleasure in "thinking," and often burn their candle of life at both ends, because of this tendency; and incline to occupations in which their brains rather than their body is exercised. They may be either of dark or of light complexion, and in either case are apt to have bright, expressive eyes. The impression created by an examination of their physical characteristics is that of *sharpness*. The fox, weasel, greyhound, and similar animals illustrate this type. Persons of this temperament are apt to be either *very* good or *very* bad. They run to extremes, and sometimes execute a quick "right about face." When properly balanced, this temperament produces the world's greatest thinkers along all lines of thought. When not properly balanced it produces the abnormally gifted "genius," between whom and the unbalanced person there is but a slender line of division; or the eccentric person with his so-called "artistic temperament," the "crank" with his hobbies and vagaries, and the brilliant degenerate who dazzles yet horrifies the world.

BALANCED TEMPERAMENTS

The best authorities agree in the belief that the Balanced Temperament is the most desirable. That is, the condition in which the three temperaments balance each other perfectly, so that the weak points of each are remedied by the strong points of the others, and the extremes of each are neutralized and held in check by the influence of the others. Prof. O. S. Fowler, the veteran phrenologist says upon this point: "A well balanced organism, with all the temperaments large and in about equal proportion, is by far the best and most favorable for both enjoyment and efficiency; to general genius and real greatness; to strength along with perfection of character; to consistency and power throughout. The Motive large, with the Mental deficient, gives power with sluggishness, so that the powers lie dormant; adding large Vital gives great physical power and enjoyment, with too little of the Mental and the moral, along with coarseness; while the Mental in excess creates too much mind for body, too much exquisiteness and sentimentality for the stamina, along with a green-house precocity most destructive of life's powers and pleasures; whereas their equal balance gives abundance of vital force; physical stamina, and mental power and susceptibility. They may be compared to the several parts of a steamboat and its appurtenances. The Vital is the steam-power; the Motive, the hulk or framework; the Mental, the freight or passengers. Predominant Vital generates more vital energy than can well be worked off, which causes restlessness, excessive passion, and a pressure which endangers outbursts and overt actions; predominant Motive gives too much frame or hulk, moves slowly, and with weak Mental, is too light-freighted to secure the great ends of life, predominant Mental overloads, and endangers sinking; but all equally balanced and powerful, carry great loads rapidly and well, and accomplish wonders. Such persons unite cool judgments with intense and well-governed feelings; great force of character and intellect with perfect consistency; scholarship with sound common sense; far seeing sagacity with brilliancy; and have the highest order of both physiology and mentality."

Professor Nelson Sizer, another high authority said: "In nature the temperaments exist in combination, one being, however, the most conspicuous. So rarely do we find examples of an even mixture or balance, that it may be said that they who possess it are marvellous exceptions in the current of human society. Such an even mixture would indicate a most extraordinary heritage; it would be constitutional perfection. But, once in a while, a person is met in whom there is a close approach to this balance, and we are accustomed to speak of it as a *balanced* temperament, it being difficult to determine which element is in predominance.

MIXED TEMPERAMENTS

The experience of the older phrenologists, which is verified by the investigations of the later authorities, was that in the majority of persons *two* of the temperaments are well developed, the third remaining comparatively undeveloped. Of the two active temperaments, *one* is usually found to be predominant, although in many the two are found to be almost equally developed. But even in the last mentioned instance one of the two seems to have been more actively called forth by the environment of the person, and may therefore be regarded as the ruling temperament. Arising from this fact we find the several classes of Mixed Temperament, known, respectively, as: the Vital-Motive; the Motive-Vital; the Motive-Mental; the Mental-Motive; the Vital-Mental; and the Mental-Vital. In these classes the name of the predominant, or most active temperament appears first, the second name indicating the temperament relatively undeveloped or inactive.

The *Vital-Motive* and the *Motive-Vital* temperaments give the combination in which is manifested physical activity and strong vitality. . Those of these temperaments are adapted to out-of-door work, such as farming, out-of-door trades, mechanics, soldiers and sailors, and other occupations requiring strong vital power and muscular strength and activity. The physical characteristics are the prominent bones and strong muscles of the Motive, and well-rounded limbs and "stout" forms of the Vital. When the Vital predominates, there is apt to be more flesh; when the Motive predominates there is apt to be more ruggedness and muscular development.

The *Motive-Mental* and *Mental-Motive* temperaments give the combination in which is manifested the physical activity of the Motive and the mental activity of the Motive and the mental activity of the Mental—the physical and mental characteristics of the

Vital being absent. The Mental element relieves the Motive of some of its crudeness and roughness, while the Motive relieves the Mental of its tendency to get away from the practical side of things. The strong frame and muscles are balanced by the brain-development. Those of this temperament make good practical business men, physicians, lawyers, scientists, explorers, and others who have to work and think at the same time. These people often manifest great executive ability. When the Motive predominates, the tendency is toward out-of-door occupations in which the brain is used in connection with bodily activity. When the Mental predominates there is a tendency toward in-door occupations in which active brain work is required. These people have well-developed heads, together with wiry, strong bodies. Some of the most successful men have come from this class.

The *Vital-Mental* and *Mental-Vital* temperaments give the combination in which is manifested many attractive traits which render their possessor agreeable, companionable, and at the same time bright and intelligent. The Vital element gives a plumpness to the form, while the Mental imparts a brightness to the mind. This is the temperament of many attractive women. The Mental activity tends to counterbalance the Vital tendency toward physical ease and comfort. These people make good orators, after dinner speakers, and agreeable society men and women, actors, artists, poets, and popular literary men. The respective predominance of the Mental or the Vital, in this combination, gives to this class somewhat of a variety, but a little observation will soon enable one to recognize the individuals belonging to it. A certain combination in this class produces the trait of "emotionality," or superficial feeling and sympathy.

The student of Human Nature should pay much attention to Temperament and the outward indications of each class and sub-class, for Temperament gives us much of our best information regarding character and disposition, in fact Character Reading depends materially upon the interpretation of Temperament.

CHAPTER V

THE MENTAL QUALITIES

We now approach the subject of the several particular mental qualities, and the groups thereof, both in the phase of their inner states and that of their outer form. In the consideration of both of these phases we must avail ourselves of the investigations and researches of the old phrenologists who cleared a path for all who follow. Although many of the phrenological theories are rejected by modern psychologists and biologists, nevertheless their work established a firm foundation for the science of the study of the brain and its functions. And to Gall and his followers we are indebted for the discovery and teaching that the activity and development of the several mental qualities or faculties manifest in outer form in the shape of the skull.

The general principles of phrenology may be briefly stated as follows:

I. The Brain is the organ of the mind.

II. The mind is not a single entity or power, but has several faculties, stronger or

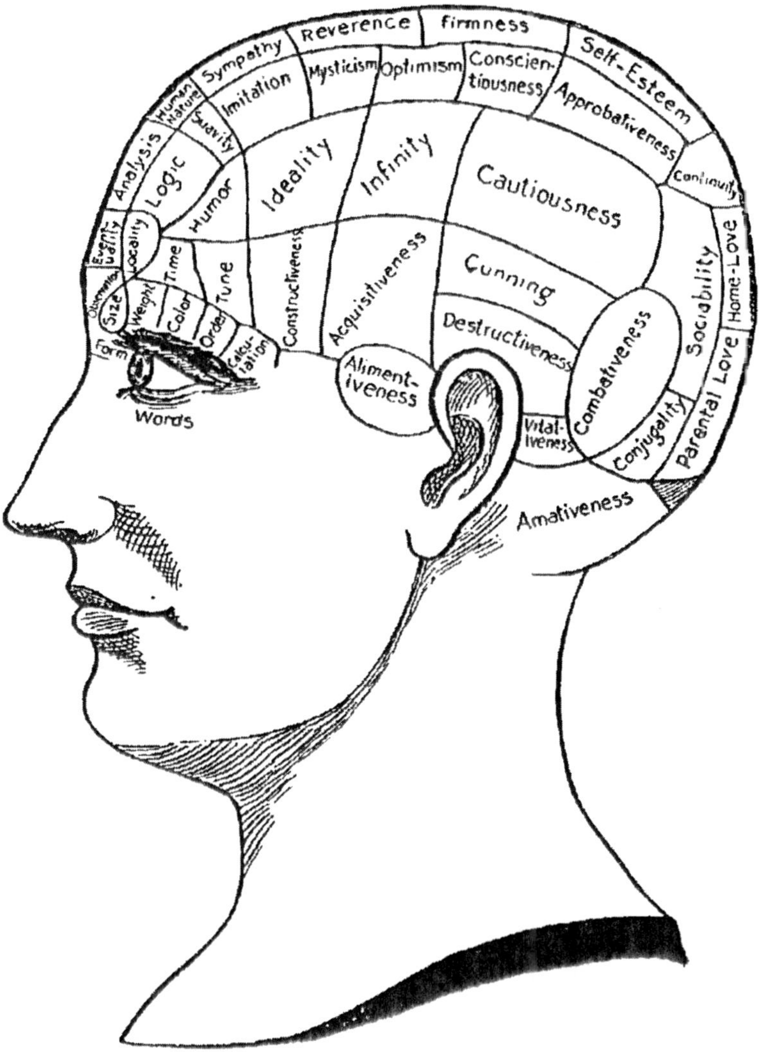

FIG. 1

THE MENTAL QUALITIES

weaker, which determine the character of the individual.

III. That each faculty or propensity has a special organ in the brain.

IV. The size of the brain (the quality being equal) is the true measure of power.

V. There are several groups of faculties, and each group is represented by organs located in the same region of the brain.

VI. The relative size of each organ results from the activity of its appropriate faculty.

VII. The size of the organ is indicated by the appearance and size of the skull immediately over the region of the organ.

VIII. The Quality and Temperament of the organization determine the degree of vigor, activity, and endurance of the mental powers.

Modern psychology and biology claim to have disproven many of the phrenological contentions, while other lines of investigation have given us other theories to account for the phenomena first noted by the phrenologists. Some investigators of brain development and action hold that while certain mental states manifest in outer form on portions of the skull, the phenomenon is due to the action of the *cranial muscles* rather than to the fact of the localization of special faculties—that each mental state is associated with certain actions on the part of certain cranial muscles which in turn exert a modifying effect upon the shape and size of the skull.

As Erbes states it "the effect the scheme of cranial muscles have had and still have upon the conformation of the skull, and, consequently, had in determining the location of those areas and in giving brain and mind a character approximately identical from end to end of the scale of living things possessing the cerebro-spinal nervous system. In so far as the neural matter is dependent upon the cranial muscles—aside from the sensory stimuli—so far, likewise are the psychic manifestations, through tongue or limb, modified by variations in those muscles that, after their creative task is done, assume a vaso-motor control over their respective areas." The same writer also says: "The cerebral mass owes its location and subsequent expansion, moreover, in a measure that mind owes its character, primarily to the action of the muscles attached to and lying upon its peripheral covering, the skull; these same muscles thereafter, through exercising a cerebral vasomotor control, act in the nature of keys for calling the evolved dependent brain areas into play, singly and en masse.''

Others have held that the development of certain areas of the surface of the skull is due to peculiar neural or nervous, activities having their seat in certain parts of the brain adjacent to their appropriate area of the skull, but these theories fail to explain the nature of the relation between the mind, brain and the ''nerve centres'' aforesaid.

These several authorities, and others, however, agree upon the fact that certain areas of the brain are associated in some way with certain mental states; and that these brain areas register their relative activity upon the areas of the skull adjacent thereto; and that the *activity* and *power* of each brain area, or faculty, is denoted by the *size* of the associated skull-area. Thus, the outward facts claimed by phrenology are admitted, while their theories of cause are disputed.

In this book we shall rest content with these "outward facts" of phrenology, and shall not concern ourselves with the various theories which seek to explain them, preferring to leave that task for others. In considering the subject of the Outer Form associated with the Inner State of Human Nature, we shall merely claim that *mental states manifest in outer form in the shape and size of the head; and that certain areas of the skull are thus associated with certain mental states, the size and shape of the former denoting the degree of activity of the latter.*

The general scheme of classification of the various mental "faculties" of the phrenologists, and the names given thereto by the old phrenologists, have in the main been adhered to in this book. In a number of cases, however, we have seen fit to re-arrange the groups in accordance with the later ideas of the New Psychology, and have given to some of the "faculties" names considered more appropriate to the later classification, and understanding of the mental state. Moreover, in order to avoid the phrenological theories attaching thereto, we have decided not to use the terms, "faculties," "propensities," and "sentiments," in referring to the several mental states; and shall therefore use the term "*Qualities*" in the place thereof. The term "quality," while denoting "the condition of being such or such; nature relatively considered," does not carry with it the theory attached to the phrenological term "faculty." But the *locality* of the several qualities of "faculties" has not been disturbed or changed—the *place* where each quality *manifests in outer form*, as assigned in this book, agrees with that assigned by the old phrenologists, time having served to establish the truth of the same, rather than to disprove it.

The following is the classification and terminology adopted by us in this book in the consideration of the Mental Qualities. (See Fig. 1.)

I. THE EGOISTIC QUALITIES: Self-Esteem; and Approbativeness.

II. THE MOTIVE QUALITIES: Combativeness; Destructiveness; Cunning; Cautiousness; Acquisitiveness; and Constructiveness.

III. THE VITATIVE QUALITIES: Vitativeness; Alimentativeness; and Bibativeness.

IV. THE EMOTIVE QUALITIES: Amativeness; Conjugality; Parental Love; Sociability and Home-Love.

V. THE APPLICATIVE QUALITIES: Firmness; and Continuity.

VI. THE MODIFICATIVE QUALITIES: Ideality; Infinity; and Humor.

VII. THE RELATIVE QUALITIES: Human Nature; Suavity; Sympathy; and Imitation.

VIII. THE PERCEPTIVE QUALITIES: Observation; Form; Size; Weight; Color; Order; Calculation; Tune; Time; Locality; Eventuality; and Words.

IX. THE REFLECTIVE QUALITIES: Analysis; and Logic.

X. THE RELIGIO-MORAL QUALITIES: Reverence; Mysticism; Optimism; and Conscientiousness.

In the following several chapters we shall consider each group, in turn, together with the particular Qualities of each group. *It must be remembered that the power of each Quality is modified by the influence of the other Qualities. Therefore in judging the character of an individual, each and every Quality must be taken into consideration.*

CHAPTER VI

THE EGOISTIC QUALITIES

The first group of Qualities is that known as the Egoistic Qualities, which is composed of two particular Qualities, known, respectively, as *Self-Esteem;* and *Approbativeness.* This group manifests outer form immediately at the "crown" of the head, and on the sides directly beneath or "side of" the crown. (See Fig. 2.) It is the seat of the consciousness of Individuality and Personality, and the tendencies arising directly therefrom.

SELF-ESTEEM. This Quality manifests in a strong sense of individual power, self-respect, self-help, self-reliance, dignity, complacency, pride of individuality, and independence. In excess it tends to produce egotism, abnormal conceit, imperiousness, etc. Deficiency of it is apt to produce lack of confidence in self, humility, self-depreciation, etc. It gives to one the ambitious spirit, and the desire for executive positions and places of authority. It resents assumption of au-

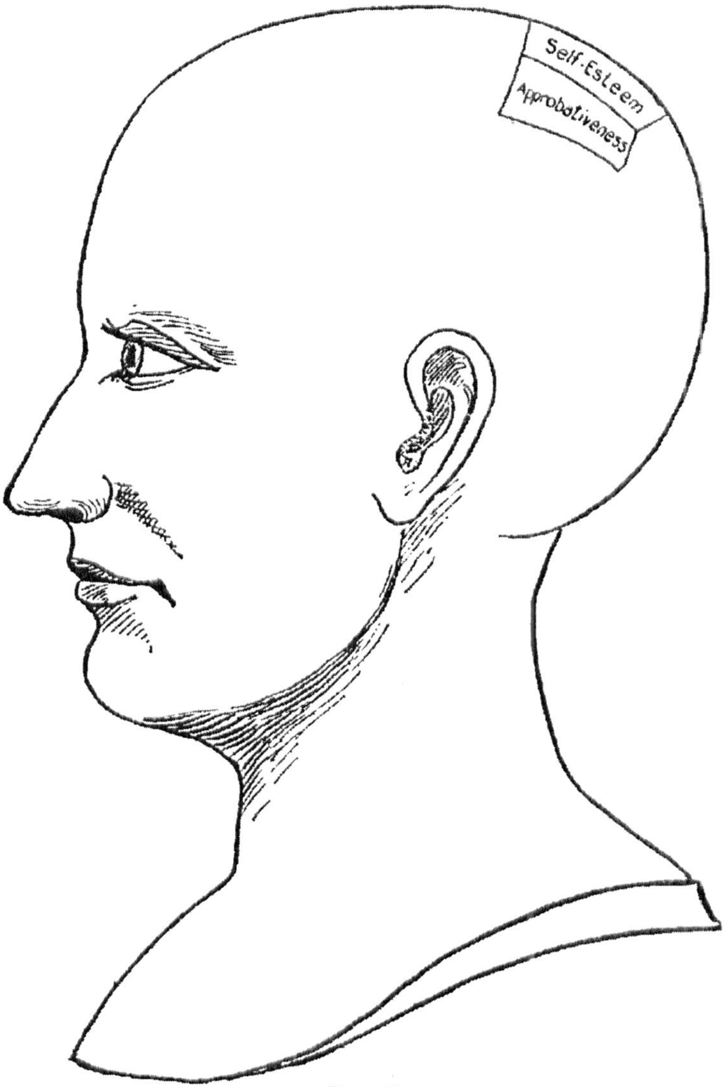

FIG. 2
THE EGOISTIC QUALITIES

thority on the part of others, and chafes under restraint. It renders its possessors dignified and desirous of the respectful recognition of others. It manifests outer form on the middle line of the head, at the "crown" (see group figure) just above Approbativeness, where it may be perceived by reason of the enlargement of the "crown." When fully developed, it tends to draw back the head, so that the latter is held erect; whereas, when deficient it allows the head to droop forward in an attitude lacking the appearance of pride.

APPROBATIVENESS. This Quality manifests in a strong desire for praise, approval, flattery, recommendation, fame, notoriety, good name, personal display, show and outward appearance. It is a form of pride different from that of Self-Esteem, for it is a vanity arising from personal things and outward appearances, whereas Self-Esteem gives a pride to the inner self or ego. Those in whom it is well-developed pay great attention to outward form, ceremony, etiquette, fashion, and social recognition, and are always to be found on the popular side and "with the crowd." They thrive upon praise, approval and notoriety, and shrink under censure, disapproval or lack of notice. One with Self-Esteem can be happy when alone, and in fact often defies public opinion and fashion from very pride of self; while one with Approbativeness largely developed lacks the pride to rise above approval and the opinion of others, while possessing a strong sense of vanity when public favor is bestowed. It manifests outer form at the upper-back part of the head, just above Cautiousness and below Self-Esteem, (see group figure). When largely developed it rises like two mounts on either side of Self-Esteem, but when Self-Esteem is large and Approbativeness is small, the latter appears as two sunken places on either side of Self-Esteem.

Self-Esteem values the *real self* while Approbativeness values the *appearances* of personality. The one pursues the substance, the other the shadows. Self-Esteem and Approbativeness are often confused in the minds of the public. The true keynote of the first is Pride; of the second, Vanity. The student should learn to carefully distinguish between these two Qualities. Approbativeness may cause one to make a monkey of himself in order to win notice, praise or laughter, while Self-Esteem will never sacrifice self-respect and pride in order to win applause.

CHAPTER VII

THE MOTIVE QUALITIES

The second group is known as the Selfish Qualities, and is composed of the following particular Qualities: *Combativeness; Destructiveness; Cunning; Cautiousness; Acquisitiveness* and *Constructiveness.* This group manifests in outer form extending along the sides of the lower head from the back toward the temples. (See Fig. 3.)

COMBATIVENESS. This Quality manifests in a strong desire to oppose, resist, combat, defy, defend. Those in whom it is developed enjoy a "scrap," and, in the words of the familiar saying, would "rather fight than eat." When combined with Vitativeness it manifests in the tendency to fight hard for life. When combined with Acquisitiveness it manifests in the tendency to fight for money or property. When combined with Amativeness it manifests in the tendency to fight for mates. When combined with the family-loving Qualities it manifests in a tendency to fight for the family. In fact, its particular

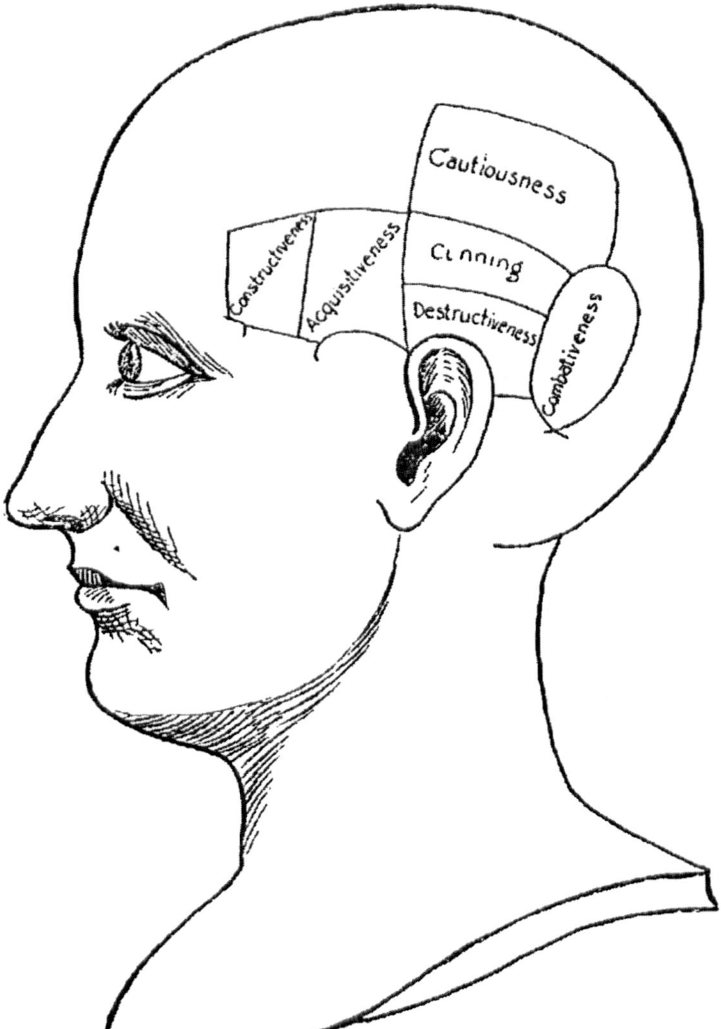

Fig. 3

THE MOTIVE QUALITIES

direction is indicated by the development and combination of the other Qualities. It manifests in outer form at the sides of the lower-back part of the head, a little back of the top part of the ear (see group figure), giving, when developed, enlargement of that part of the head—a "broad back-head." The "broad-headed" animals, birds, and fish have this propensity well developed, while the "narrow-heads" have it in but a small degree. It is also indicated by the strong jaw, and by the mouth indicating a "strong bite."

DESTRUCTIVENESS. This Quality, manifests in a strong desire to break precedents, doing things in new ways, asserting authority, extermination, severity, sternness, breaking down, crushing, "walking over," etc. Its direction is largely governed by the other Qualities, as for instance in combination with Acquisitiveness, it manifests in breaking down opposition and precedents in business; while with large conscientiousness it manifests in tearing down evil conditions, etc., and in doing the work of "reform." It generally is accompanied with large Combativeness, as the two go hand-in-hand. It manifests outer form directly above, and back of the top-part of the ear (see group figure).

CUNNING. This Quality manifests in a strong desire to be cunning, sly, close-mouthed, diplomatic, deceitful, and generally "foxy." It is best illustrated by the example of the fox, which animal combines in itself many of its qualities. The coyote also shows signs of having this Quality well developed, as do birds of the crow and blackbird family, and certain fishes. With strong Caution it renders one very secretive and "close-mouthed." With strong Acquisitiveness it renders one sly and tricky in business. With strong Approbativeness it renders one apt to tell lying stories which magnify his importance and gratify his vanity. With a vivid Imagination it inclines one to draw on that quality and lie for the very love of romancing. It manifests outer form a little distance above the top of the ear, immediately above Destructiveness, and back of Acquisitiveness (see group figure).

CAUTIOUSNESS. This Quality manifests in a strong desire to avoid danger or trouble; carefulness, prudence, watchfulness, anxiety, self-protection, etc. In excess it is apt to render one fearful, over-anxious, and even cowardly, but in combination with other Qualities it tends to give to one a balance and to restrain him from rashness and unnecessary risk. Its direction is also largely influenced by the development of other Qualities. Thus with large Acquisitiveness it makes one very cautious about money matters; with large family qualities it renders one very careful about the family; with large Approbativeness it renders one bashful, self conscious, and fearful of adverse criticism. It manifests outer form toward the upper-back part of the head, directly over Secretiveness (see group figure), and when developed is apparent by the enlargement of the comparatively large area covered by it. An old phrenological authority says of it: "This is the easiest found of all the organs. . . . Starting at the middle of the back part of the ears, draw a perpendicular line, when the head is erect, straight up to where the head begins to slope back in forming the top, and Caution is located just at the first turn."

ACQUISITIVENESS. This Quality manifests

in a strong desire either to acquire, or else to hold property, money, or general objects of possession. In some cases it contents itself with merely "getting," while in others it also "holds on" to what is secured, the difference arising from the combinations of the other Qualities. In itself, it may be said to be merely the tendency toward "hoarding up," but the combination with large Combativeness and Destructiveness enlarges its scope and tends to make its possessor rapacious and grasping. It is the instinct of the squirrel and the bee, and even the dog manifests it when he buries a bone for future gnawing purposes. Those in whom it is developed in connection with large Caution, manifest a strict economy and even miserliness, while in others it expends itself in merely the getting for the sake of the getting, the possessions often being scattered prodigally afterward, the element of Approbativeness entering largely into the latter action. It manifests outer form in the lowest-middle section of the head, directly over Alimentiveness (see group figure).

CONSTRUCTIVENESS. This Quality manifests in a strong desire to invent, construct, build, create, put together, improve upon, add to, readjust, etc. It manifests along three general lines, namely (1) Invention; (2) Construction; and (3) Materialization, by which is meant the "making real" of *ideals* previously entertained—the "making come true" of the dreams previously experienced—the *materialization* of the ideas, plans, and projects previously *visualized.* This Quality causes the person to improve, alter, tinker with, build up, invent, and create along the lines of his vocation or avocation. These people find it difficult to refrain from tinkering with, altering, or "improving" anything and everything with which they have to do. With large Logic, Analysis, and Perceptives they manifest inventive ability; with large Imitation they are fond of copying and constructing after models; with large Ideality they work toward making their dreams come true. This Quality is not confined to mechanical construction, as the old phrenologists taught, but manifests itself in business literature, art, and in fact in every vocation or occupation. With large Destructiveness, it builds up new structures upon the ruins created by that Quality. In persons of the Motive temperament it inclines toward mechanical invention, creation and construction; while in persons of the Mental temperament it manifests in creating and constructing ideas, thoughts, theories, scientific classification, literary productions, etc., and in persons of the Vital temperament it manifests in creating and improving upon things calculated to appeal to persons of that class. It manifests outer form in the lower and frontal part of the temples, backward and upward from the outer corner of the eye-brow (see group figure). Prof. O. S. Fowler says. "In broad-built and stocky persons it causes this part of the temples to widen and bulge out, but in tall, long-headed persons it *spreads* out upon them, and hence shows to be less than it really is." It is directly below Ideality and in front of Acquisitiveness.

CHAPTER VIII

THE VITATIVE QUALITIES

The third group is known as the Vitative Qualities, which is composed of the three respective particular Qualities: *Vitativeness; Alimentativeness;* and *Bibativeness*. This group manifests in outer form directly back of, and in front of, the middle part of the ear. (See Fig. 4.)

VITATIVENESS. This quality manifests in a strong desire to live; resistance to disease and death; an intense clinging to life for the mere fact of living, rather than for the sake of anything to be accomplished by continued existence. It goes along with Combativeness, and is especially noticeable in the "broad-headed" people and animals. The cat tribe, hawks, turtles, sharks, venomous snakes, and others have this propensity well developed, while it is deficient in the "narrow-headed" animals, such as the rabbit, certain birds, certain fish, and many harmless snakes. Those in whom it is developed "die hard," while those in whom it is deficient die easily. This

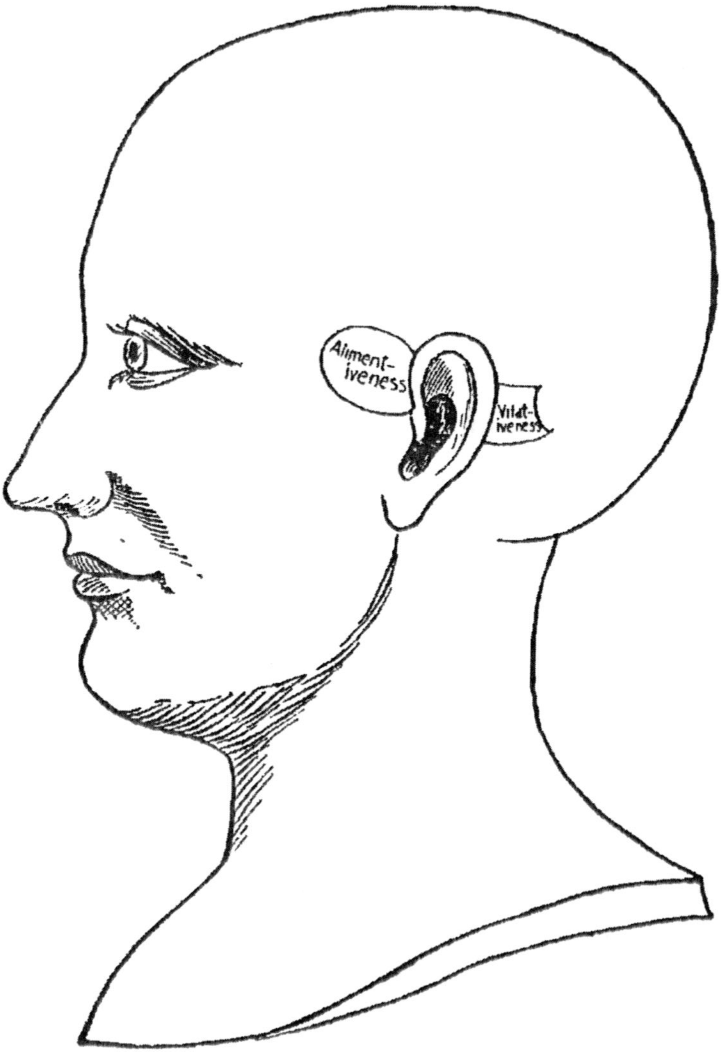

Fig. 4
THE VITATIVE QUALITIES

capacity manifests in outer form in the area situated just back of the middle part of the ear (see group figure).

ALIMENTIVENESS. This Quality manifests in a strong desire to gratify the tastes for food, when large it inclines one toward gluttony, and tends to make one "live to eat," instead of to "eat to live." Those in whom it is largely developed eat heartily and like to see others doing the same; while those in whom it is deficient care very little for the quality or amount of their food and often actually resent the, to them, "disgusting" sight of persons partaking of a hearty meal. It manifests in outer form immediately in front of the upper part of the ear (see group figure).

BIBATIVENESS. This Quality manifests in a strong desire to gratify the appetite for drinks of various kinds. In its normal well-developed state it manifests in a desire for water, milk and fluid foods, such as soups, broths, etc., and other juicy things. Perverted it manifests in the appetite for intoxicating liquors, tea and coffee, "soft drinks," and the various decoctions of the modern soda-fountain. By some this Quality is regarded as merely a phase of Alimentiveness, while others consider it to be a separate Quality. It manifests in outer form immediately in front of the locality of Alimentiveness, toward the eye.

CHAPTER IX

THE EMOTIVE QUALITIES

The fourth group is that known as the Social Qualities, which group is composed of the following particular Qualities: *Amativeness; Conjugality; Parental Love; Sociability* and *Home Love.* This group manifests outer form at the lower-back portion of the head (see Fig. 5), and shows itself by an enlargement of that region, causing the head to "bulge" back of the ears. It may best be understood by an examination of its several particular Qualities.

Amativeness. This Quality manifests in a strong desire for sexual indulgence and association with the opposite sex. Its purpose is, of course, the reproduction of the race, but its abuse and perversion has led man to many excesses and unnatural practices. It is a dynamic propensity and its normal development is seemingly necessary in order to produce the "life spirit," and vital activity mental and physical. Those in whom it is deficient lack "spirit" and energy, while those

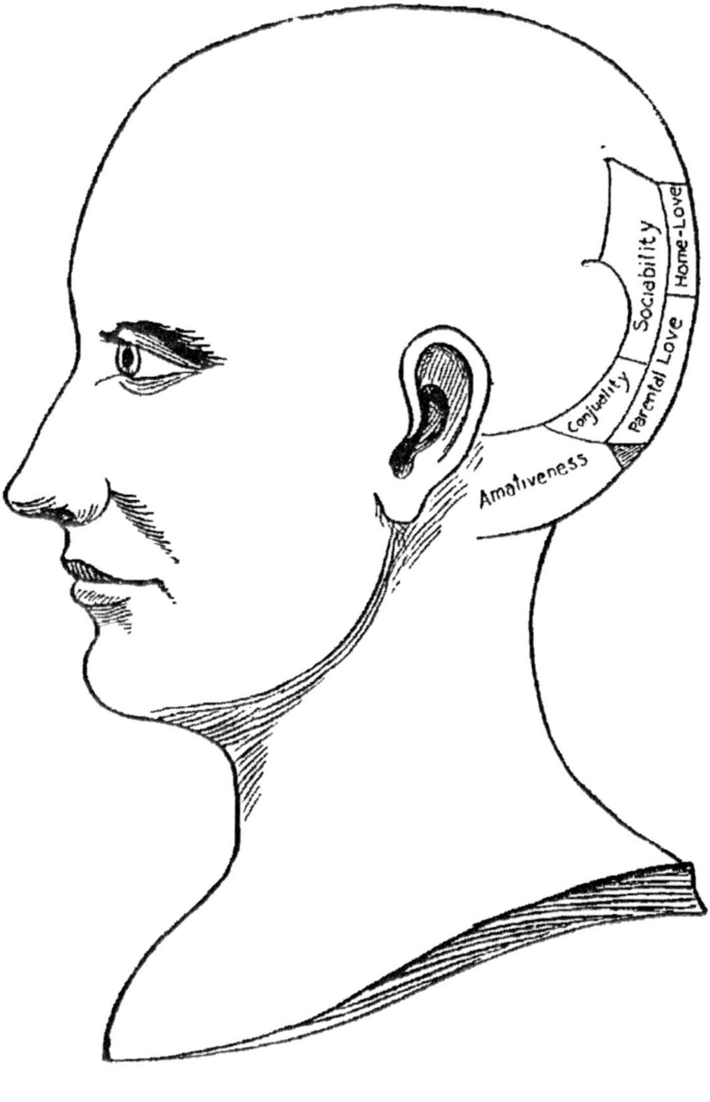

FIG. 5
THE EMOTIVE QUALITIES

in whom it is developed to excess tend to lean toward excesses. When developed normally it seems to add an attractiveness or "magnetism" to its possessors; when deficient it renders the person "cold" non-magnetic and unattractive; when over-developed and unrestrained it causes the person to become disgusting and repulsive to the normal person; vulgar, licentious and depraved. Its seat is in the cerebellum or "little brain," and it manifests outer form by an enlarged "fullness" at the nape of the neck, at the base of the skull (see group figure). It tends to cause the head to lean backward and downward at the nape of the neck. It also manifests by fullness of the lips, particularly in their middles. The lips and position of the head of persons in whom this quality is largely developed is indicative of the attitude and position of kissing. Spurzheim says of it: "It is situated at the top of the neck, and its size is proportionate to the space between the mastoid process, immediately behind the ears, and the occipital spine, in the middle of the hind head." It is noticeable that those in whom this quality is fully or largely developed seem to have the power of attracting or "charming" those of the opposite sex, while those who are deficient in it lack this quality.

CONJUGALITY. This quality manifests in a strong desire for a "mate"—and *one* mate only. While Amativeness may cause one to seek the society of many of the opposite sex, Conjugality will act only to cause one to seek the *one* life partner. Conjugality causes the desire to "mate for life." It is something quite different from Amativeness, although of course related to it. The location of its outer form, between Amativeness and Friendship, gives the key to its quality—*love with companionship*. Those in whom it is well developed are very close to their mates and tend toward jealousy; they suffer intensely when the relation is inharmonious or disturbed in any way, and are often broken-hearted at disappointment in love or the death of the mate. Those in whom it is deficient feel very little true companionship for their mates, and with Amativeness large are apt to be promiscuous in their manifestation of love or passion; if one love is interrupted or interfered with they find little difficulty in shifting their affections. Those in whom it is strong are "true unto death," while those in whom it is weak are fickle, inconstant and lack loyalty. The Quality manifests outer form on each side of the lower-back of the head, just above Amativeness and just below Friendship, and on either side of Parental Love—the location being especially indicative of its nature (see group figure).

PARENTAL LOVE. This Quality manifests in a strong desire for and love of children, particularly one's own. Those in whom it is very strong often adopt children in addition to their own and love to caress children wherever and whenever they may see them. It manifests outer form at the lower-back part of the head on the middle-line of the head, above Amativeness, and below Inhabitiveness (see group figure).

SOCIABILITY. This Quality manifests in a strong desire for companionship, fellowship, friends, sympathy, society, associates, etc. It is the "social sense." Those in whom it is strong feel happy only when surrounded by associates, friends or boon companions.

They incline toward lodges, clubs and social gatherings. To be alone is to suffer, to such people. Those in whom it is weak prefer to be alone, or at the best with a few carefully chosen companions, and avoid promiscuous friendships and social gatherings. It manifests outer form just above Conjugality, and at the sides of Parental love and Inhabitiveness, and directly back of Cautiousness and the upper-part of Combativeness (see group figure).

HOME-LOVE. This Quality manifests in a strong love of familiar places, particularly of one's home and near-by country, and from this springs love of country and patriotism. Those in whom it is strong dislike to travel, and are subject to home-sickness. Those in whom it is weak are fond of travel, readily change their places of abode, and are apt to become "roamers" if they indulge the Quality. When over large, it inclines one toward narrowness, sectionalism and provincialism; when small, it inclines one toward frequent moves, and changes of residence and location. It manifests outer form at the back part of the head, on the middle-line, directly above Parental Love and below Continuity (see group figure). When it is large it tends to produce a ridge, flat-iron-shape and pointing upward; when small, it presents a depression sufficient to contain the ball of the finger. Its close connection to Continuity, on the one hand, and Parental Love on the other, is very suggestive.

CHAPTER X

THE APPLICATIVE QUALITIES

The fifth group, known as the Applicative Qualities, is composed of two particular Qualities, known, respectively, as *Firmness* and *Continuity*. This group manifests in outer form on the centre-line of the head, just above and just below the "crown," at which latter point Self-Esteem is situated (see Fig. 6).

FIRMNESS. This Quality manifests in a strong tendency toward stability, tenacity, fixedness of purpose, and decision. When very highly developed with the reasoning powers weak it often manifests as stubborness, mulishness, obstinacy, etc. Those in whom it is largely developed display firmness in decision, are "set in their ways," cannot be driven by force or converted by argument when they have once formed an opinion and taken a stand. The "indomitable will" arises from this Quality, in fact this Quality might well be termed the "Will Quality," although it manifests by that as-

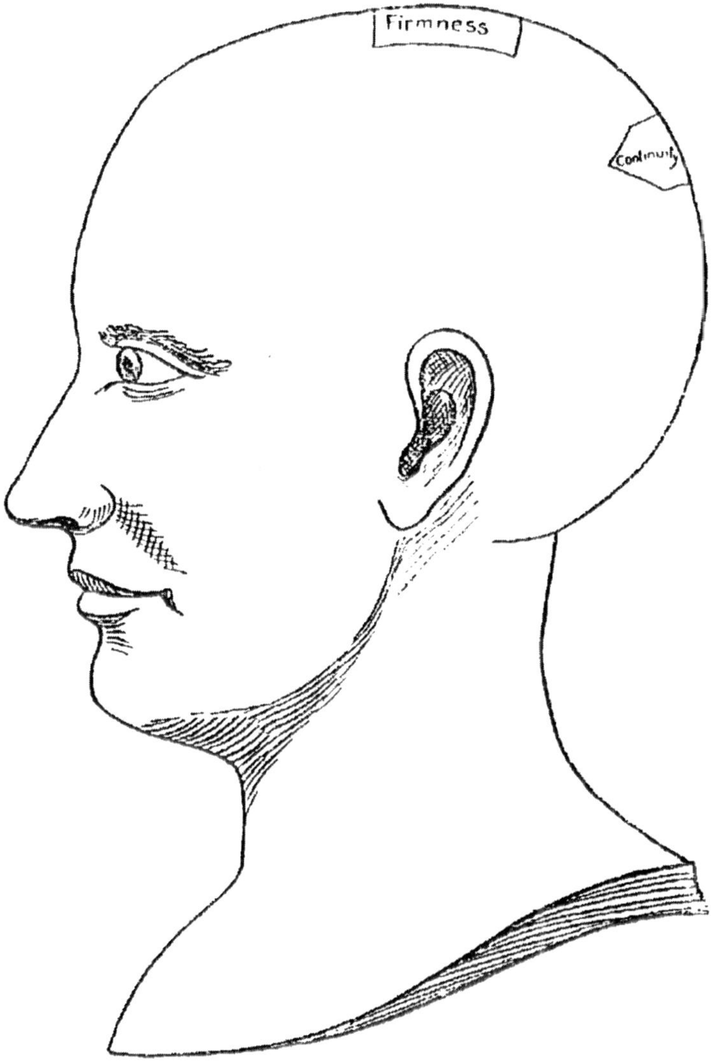

FIG. 6
THE APPLICATIVE QUALITIES

pect of Will which shows itself as *fixedness*, while its companion Quality, that of Continuity, manifests the phase of Will known as "stick-to-it-iveness." Persons in whom Firmness is largely developed make certain decisions and then abide by them. They may be coaxed but never driven. Prof. O. S. Fowler, speaking of this Quality, said: "No man ever succeeded without great will-power to hold on and hold out in the teeth of opposing difficulties. I never knew a man distinguished for anything, not even crimes, to lack it. It is an indispensable prerequisite of greatness and goodness. Without it great talents are of little avail, for they accomplish little; but with it large, fair to middling capacities accomplish commendable results. Success in life depends more on this than on any other single attribute."

This Quality manifests outer form on the centre-line of the back part of the top head, just above Self-Esteem. The location may be ascertained by holding the head erect, drawing an imaginary line upward from the opening of the ears straight to the top of the head to the middle-line or centre of the top of the head—the location is at this last-point. It is usually quite prominent, and in many men unusually large. When fully developed it gives a "tallness" to the head from the opening of the ears to top of head. When it is weak, there is apt to be a flatness or even a depression at the point of its location. It also manifests in a "stiff upper lip," that is a firm upper lip, the latter often being longer than ordinarily. A certain stiffness of the upper-lip is often noticed when Firmness is habitually asserted, or in cases when the Quality is temporarily called into play. The term "stiff upper lip" is more than a mere figurative expression. Combe says of this Quality: "When this organ predominates it gives a peculiar hardness to the manner, a stiffness and uprightness to the gait, with a forcible and emphatic tone to the voice."

CONTINUITY. This propensity manifests in a strong tendency to "stick-to" a thing once begun, until it is finished; a disinclination for change; a habit of patient work and thought; a desire to do but one thing at a time; etc. It is difficult to interest these people in *new* things—they hold fast to the *old*. They are naturally conservative and are averse to "new-fangled" things. They are plodders and steady workers, and run on like a clock when once wound up. They are apt to possess the power of long and continued concentration upon anything which attracts their attention, although it is difficult to attract their attention to an entirely new thing. Prof. Sizer says: "Firmness gives a stiff, determined fortitude, decision of character; it serves to brace up the other faculties to the work in hand. . . . Firmness gives determination and obstinacy of purpose, while *Continuity* gives a patient, perfecting, plodding application. Of two stone-cutters with equal Firmness, they will be alike thorough and persevering, but if one has large Continuity he prefers to use the drill in one place for hours, while the other with small Continuity craves variety, and prefers to use the chisel in cutting and dressing the entire surface of the stone."

Continuity in excess often manifests in "long-windedness," prosiness, boredom, prolixity and tiresomeness. When it is weak there is manifested a "flightiness," tendency to change, lack of concentration, attraction of the new, a shifting of base, change of mind, and general instability and lack of "stick-to-itiveness." This Quality manifests outer form on the centre line of the top back of the head, just below the crown (Self-Esteem) and just above Inhabitiveness (see group figure). Reference to the group figure will show that it is peculiar in shape, and forms a semi-circular arch over a part of the top-back head. When fully developed that part of the head is simply evenly rounded with swelling; when deficient it leaves a hollow, crescent shape, horns downward. In America we find the majority of people are weak in Continuity, while in certain other countries it is found largely developed in the majority of cases. This fact gives to Americans a benefit in certain directions and a weakness in others.

Both Firmness and Continuity are manifested almost entirely in connection with the other Qualities, and are known almost altogether in that way. In themselves they have almost abstract nature. In determining character, they must be taken largely into consideration, because their influence on the other Qualities is very great. In fact they may be said to *determine* the degree of *application* of the other Qualities.

CHAPTER XI

THE MODIFICATIVE QUALITIES

The sixth group is known as the Modificative Qualities (called by the phrenologists "The Self-Perfecting Group"), which is composed of the following particular Qualities. *Ideality, Infinity,* and *Humor,* respectively. This group manifests outer form in the region of the temples, and when large gives width to the sides of the fore part of the head (See Figure 7).

IDEALITY. This Quality could well be called the "Artistic" quality of the mind. It manifests in a strong desire for the beautiful, the ideal, the elegant, the polished, the graceful, the refined. It is also closely connected with the phase of mental activity called "Imagination." Those in whom it is largely developed manifest the artistic taste and temperament, the love of art, beauty and the ideal, the poetic spirit, the love of the refined and choice—and a corresponding dislike for all opposed to these tastes and qualities.

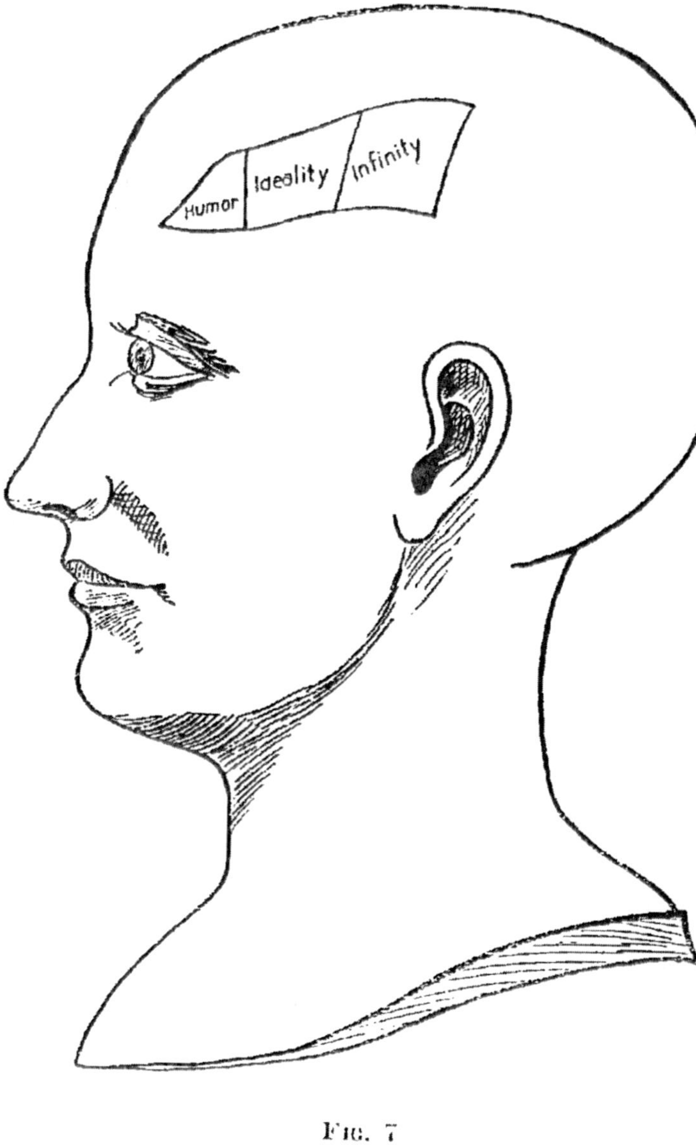

Fig. 7
THE MODIFICATIVE QUALITIES

Spurzheim says of it: "A poetic turn of mind results from a peculiar mode of feeling. Vividness, glow, exaltation, imagination, inspiration, rapture, exaggeration, and warmth of expression are requisite for poetry. Poets depict a fictitious and imaginary world. This faculty gives glow to the other faculties; impresses the poetical and ideal; aspires to imaginary perfection in every thing; creates enthusiasm in friendship, virtue, painting, music, etc.; produces sentimentality, and leads to delicacy and susceptibility. It often acts with Spirituality (Mysticism), located adjoining it, in embellishing poetry with the mysterious and supernatural. Practical exaltation varies with this organ."

Combe says: "This faculty loves exquisiteness, perfection, and the beau-ideal; gives inspiration to the poet; stimulates those faculties which form ideas to create perfect scenes; inspires man with a ceaseless love of improvement, and prompts him to form and realize splendid conceptions; imparts an elevated strain to language, and shows a splendor of eloquence and poetic feeling; and gives to conversation a fascinating sprightliness and buoyancy—the opposite of dryness and dullness.''

In addition to the above characteristics, which are largely due to the co-operation of Mysticism, Infinity, and Reverence, there is another set of manifestations which were largely overlooked by the older phrenologists —the activity of the Imagination in connection with Constructiveness. This combination of Constructiveness and Ideality is found in the great scientists, inventors, great financiers, and others whose plans for ''building up'' show that Ideality has been also very active in the direction of picturing ''what may be''—the *ideal* which Construction makes *real.* In much mental constructive work, there is found the artistic element, which arises from Ideality. This Quality manifests outer form in the upper and frontal portion of the temples, just where the head begins to curve upward, and just in front of, or under, the edges of the hair (see group figure). It is just above Constructiveness, and just below Mysticism and Imitation, a position which throws light on its several phases of manifestation above noted.

INFINITY. This Quality manifests in a strong realization of the grand, the majestic, the vast, the illimitable, the infinite, the eternal, the absolute, the omnipotent, the omnipresent, the omniscient. It is the realizing sense of The Great. Those in whom it is large are impressed by the sublime, the majestic, the grand, in nature or in thought and conception. Niagara; the great work of the architect; the thunder-storm; the giant redwood of California; the ocean; or the thoughts of Infinity, alike appeal to the one in whom this Quality is large. If Reverence be large, the trend of Infinity will be toward religious ideas—the greatness of God. If the intellectual faculties be in the ascendency, Infinity will lead to high conceptions of Space, Nature, the Infinite. If Ideality be large, Infinity will incline toward the grand and great in art. If Constructiveness be well developed, Infinity will impel to the creation of great works, enterprises, buildings, schemes, or what not. Infinity influences everything in the direction of largeness and greatness. This Quality manifests in outer form on the side of the head, about midway between forehead and back-head, and about midway between "top and bottom" of that part of the head which contains the brain (see group figure). It is back of Ideality, and in front of Cautiousness; below Optimism and above Acquisitiveness, on the side of the head where the upward curve begins.

HUMOR. This Quality manifests in a strong appreciation of the ludicrous, humorous, ironical, facetious, and raillery. Spurzheim says: "Those who write like Voltaire, Rabelais, Piron, Sterne, Rabener, Wieland, and all who are fond of jest, raillery, ridicule, irony, and comical conceptions, have the upper and outer parts of the forehead immediately before Beauty (Ideality) of considerable size." Combe says: "I have found in the manifestations of those whose Wit (Mirthfulness) predominates over Causality (Logic) a striking love of the purely ludicrous; their great delight being to heap absurd and incongruous ideas together; extract laughter out of every object; and enjoy the mirth their sallies created; and therefore agree with Spurzheim that the sentiment of the ludicrous is its primitive function." Those in whom it is very large are apt to be regarded as trifling and undignified, and people often lack respect for them. Those in whom it is weak are apt to be over-serious and dreary. A sense of humor is valuable in many ways, among which is its influence in letting us see the silly side of much pretentious nonsense which might otherwise deceive our reason and judgment. Many a solemn and dignified fallacy or error can best be attacked through a laugh and a realization of its absurdity. This Quality manifests outer form on the upper and lateral part of the forehead (see group figure). It is just before Ideality and just below Imitation. When large it gives a square and prominent shape to this part of the forehead.

CHAPTER XII

THE RELATIVE QUALITIES

The seventh group is known as the Relative Qualities, and is composed of the following four particular Qualities: *Human Nature; Suavity; Sympathy;* and *Imitation;* respectively. The designation "Relative" is applied to this group, by reason of the fact that its activities are concerned with the *relations* between the individual and others of his kind. The group manifests outer form in the front-upper part of the head, beginning just above the line of the hair, from which it extends backward toward the top-head. (See Fig. 8.)

Human Nature. This Quality manifests in a strong desire to read character, discern human motives, interpret feelings and thoughts, and to *know* men and women thoroughly. Those in whom it is large seem to read the mind, motives and character of those whom they meet, in an almost intuitive manner—the ideas, feelings, thoughts, motives and designs of others seem like an open book to them. They are natural physiognomists, and under-

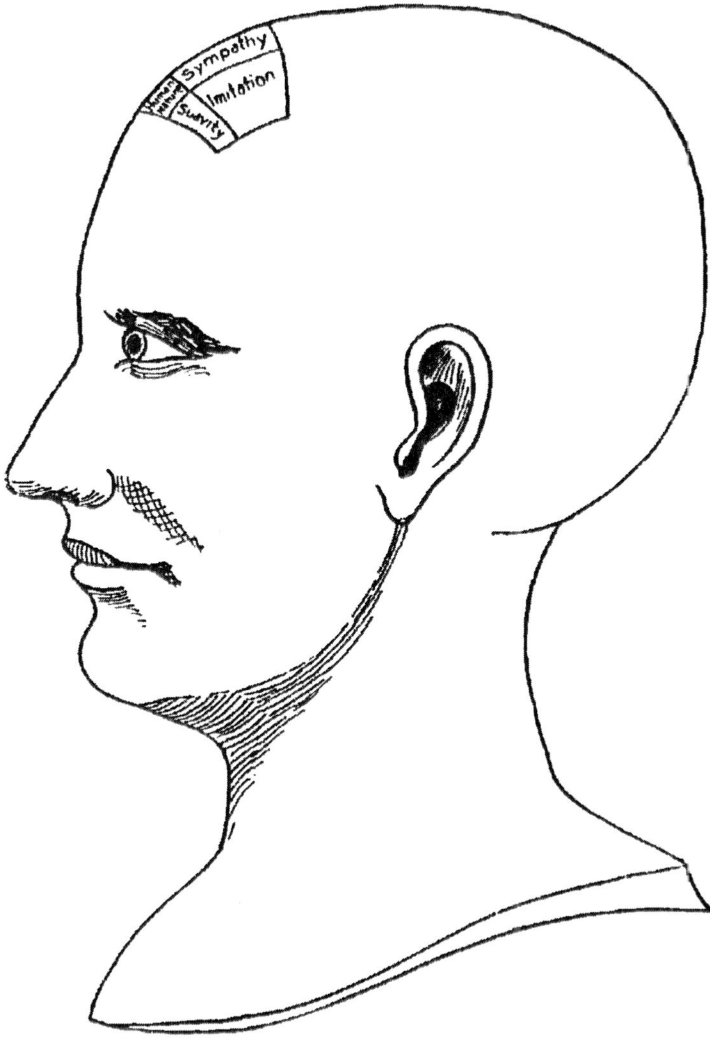

FIG. S

THE RELATIVE QUALITIES

stand Human Nature in both its inner states and outer forms. This quality is largely developed in successful salesmen, detectives, credit-men, politicians, and others whose success depends largely upon the ability to read the character of those with whom they come in contact. This Quality concerns itself with the entire subject matter of this book, and is of the utmost importance to every individual. It should be developed and trained.

Prof. O. S. Fowler explains its manifestations, and at the same time directs one along the lines of its cultivation, as follows: "Scan closely all the actions of men, in order to ascertain their motives and mainsprings of action; look with a sharp eye at man, woman and child, all you meet, as if you would read them through; note particularly the expression of the eye, as if you would imbibe what it signifies; say to yourself, what faculty prompted this expression and that action? drink in the general looks, attitude, natural language and manifestations of men, and yield yourself to the impressions naturally made on you; that is, study human nature both as a philosophy and a sentiment."

This Quality manifests in outer form on the middle-line of the summit of the forehead, just where the hair usually begins to appear, and from thence slightly upward around the curve (see group figure). It is directly above Analysis and is often mistaken for a continuation thereof. Its nearness to that Quality indicates its relationship thereto, the connection being very close; in fact, some authorities have treated it as a particular phase of Analysis. It is directly in front of and below Sympathy, which position is also suggestive, for we must first *understand* the feelings of others before we can sympathize with them. It is between the two lobes of Suavity, which position is also suggestive, for Suavity depends upon an understanding of the character and feelings of others, in order that we may "fall in" with the same. In the same way Imitation, which closely adjoins it, depends upon Human Nature for its copying material. When largely developed this Quality gives a peculiar fullness and height to the upper forehead.

SUAVITY. This Quality manifests in a strong desire to be *agreeable, suave, pleasant, polite* and *attractive* to other people. Those in whom it is large possess a charming personality; a "winning way;" are interesting and agreeable; polite, and often fascinating. They always say the right thing to the right person at the right time and right place. They sugar-coat unpleasant truths, and are natural diplomats. This is the Quality of Tact. These people are "all things to all men," and show every evidence of having "kissed the Blarney Stone," and of understanding the manufacture and use of "soft soap."

With Human Nature large, they, as Prof. O. S. Fowler says "know just how and when to take and hoodwink men; with Secretiveness (Cunning) large and Conscientiousness small, are oily and palavering, and flatter victims, and serpent-like salivate before swallowing." When the adjoining Quality of Humor is large, they add humor and wit to their other attractive qualities. This Quality, in normal development, is the lubricant which makes the wheels of social and business intercourse run smoothly. In excess it renders one "too smooth" and "oily;" while its deficiency renders one boorish, unattractive and disagreeable. It manifests in outer form in the upper-fore part of the head, about the hair-line, and *on each side of Human Nature.* It is just below Imitation, just above Logic, and touches the upper side of Mirthfulness (see group figure). Together with Human Nature, when both are large, it tends to give a squareness and fullness to the upper part of the forehead, and a somewhat angular turn to the forehead at that point.

SYMPATHY. This Quality manifests in a strong feeling of kindness, compassion, benevolence, sympathy, and desire to make and see others happy. Its manifestation is always altruistic. When largely developed it causes one to feel the pains of others, and to be unhappy at the sight, thought or hearing of their pains and woes. When deficient or weak it allows the person to be callous to the misfortunes of others. When normally developed it causes one to radiate Kindness, Sympathy and Compassion, but in excess it renders one miserable because of the consciousness of the "world-pain," and often causes one to be the victim of misplaced sympathy and confidence. It is unnecessary to state that those in whom this propensity is strong are to be found serving their fellowmen in charitable, philanthropic, and educational work. Some have it in such excess that they will impoverish themselves and their families in order to help perfect strangers or the race at large. It manifests outer form on the fore part of the top head, on the middle-line, commencing just about where the hair begins and running back almost to the middle of the top-head. It is immediately in front of Reverence. When large it tends to give the head a little forward tilt or inclination, as if toward the person for whom sympathy is felt. In listening to a story awakening sympathy, one naturally inclines the head a little forward.

IMITATION. This Quality manifests itself in the strong tendency to reproduce, copy, take pattern of, or mimic. It plays an important part in the work of the artist and the actor. It enables one in whom it is largely developed to enter into the ideas, plans and works of others; to "catch their spirit;" and to reproduce their work or ideas. In connection with Ideality it forms a large part of the artistic talent in all lines of creative work. With large Constructiveness and Ideality, it makes the inventor and the designer who build upon that which has gone before that which is new and original. With Self-Esteem small and Approbativeness large, this Quality will cause the person to "follow my leader" and imitate others, rather than to assert his own originality and creative power. This Quality is noticeable principally as a modifier of the other faculties and propensities. It manifests outer form on the upper sides of the forehead, toward the top of the head (see group figure). It lies just below Sympathy, and above Ideality; before Mysticism, and back of Suavity.

CHAPTER XIII

THE PERCEPTIVE QUALITIES

The eighth group is known as the Perceptive Qualities, composed of the following particular Qualities, respectively: *Observation; Form; Size; Weight; Color; Order; Calculation; Tune; Time; Locality; Eventuality,* and *Words.* This group manifests outer form in the lower part of the forehead, in the region of the eye. (See Fig. 9.) When large this group often gives to the upper forehead the appearance of "retreating" or sloping backward. Prof. O. S. Fowler says of the appearance of those Qualities which manifest outer form *under* the eyebrows: "The following rule for observing their size obviates the objection sometimes urged that the eyebrows and their arches prevent the correct diagnosis of these smaller organs crowded so thickly together. The rule is: *The shape of the eyebrows* reveals the size, absolute and relative, of each, thus: When *all* are large, the eyebrow is long and arching; when all are deficient, it is short and straight; when some are

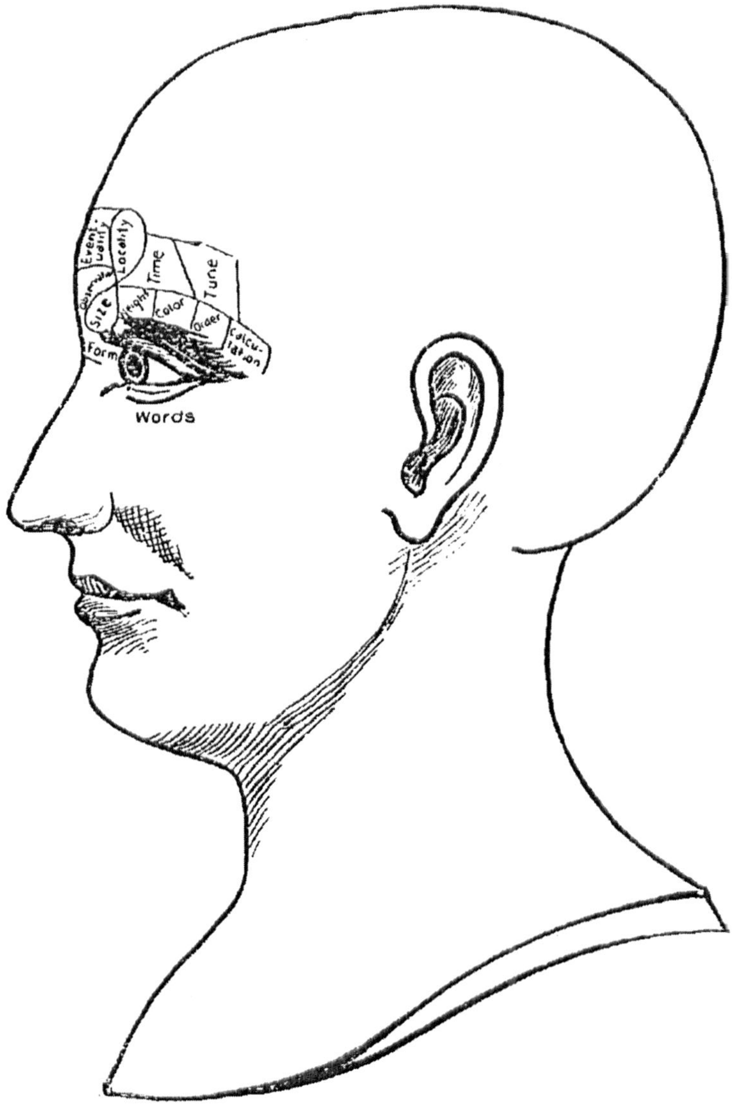

FIG. 9
THE PERCEPTIVE QUALITIES

large and others small, it arches over the large ones, but passes horizontally over those which are small. This rule is infallible." The other Qualities of the group, according to Prof. Sizer, "is located above the eyes, and . . . constitute about one-third of the depth of the forehead, beginning at the arch of the eye."

OBSERVATION. This Quality was given the name of "Individuality" by the early phrenologists, but this term is considered misleading, owing to the later usage of that term. It manifests in a strong desire to observe, see, examine, inspect, and "know" the things of the objective life. Those in whom it is largely developed feel the insatiable urge of the inquisitive spirit; they desire to investigate everything coming under their notice. Many little details in the objects or subjects in which they are interested are noticed by them, while overlooked by the majority of people.

Prof. Sizer says of it that it "gives a recognition of things and the special points and facts of subjects; quickness of observation is an important element in the acquisition of knowledge. . . . Those in whom it is large are eager to see all that may be seen, and nothing escapes their attention. It opens the door for the action of all the other perceptive organs. . . . They are quick to notice everything that is presented to the eye; and it goes farther, and enables us to recognize that which we touch, or sounds we hear. The rattling strokes of a drum are distinct noises, and each is an individuality."

Prof. O. S. Fowler, says: "It is adapted, and adapts men to the divisibility of matter, or that natural attribute which allows it to be subdivided indefinitely. Yet each division maintains a personal existence. It thus puts man in relation and contact with a world full of things for his inspection, as well as excites in him an insatiable desire to examine everything. It is therefore the *looking* faculty. Its distinctive office is to observe things. It asks: 'What is this?' and says, 'Show me that!' . . . Before we can know the uses, properties, causes, etc., of things, we must first know that such things *exist*, and of this Observation informs us."

This Quality is largely involved in the process of Attention. It usually manifests in the form of *involuntary attention,* that is, attention to interesting things. But, under the influence of the will, with Firmness large, it manifests *voluntary attention,* or attention or study of objects not interesting in themselves, but which it is important to study and know. It is largely developed in children and undeveloped adults in the phase of curiosity or desire to observe *new* things. In adults, of developed minds, it manifests as attention to things of *material interest* and important subjects or objects of study. This Quality is the master of its associated Qualities in this group, and is involved in all of their activites.

It manifests outer form in the middle of the lower part of the forehead, between the inner ends of the eyebrows, and above the top of the nose—"just above the root of the nose," in fact. Prof. O S. Fowler says: "When it is large, the eyebrows flex downward at their nasal ends, and the lower part of the forehead projects. When it is deficient, the eyebrows are straight at their inner ends, and come close together" (See group figure).

FORM. This Quality manifests in a cognizance, appreciation, and recollection of the *form and shape* of objects observed. Those in whom it is large most readily perceive, recognize and remember details of form and shape, faces, etc. It manifests outer form between, and slightly above, the eyes, on each side of Observation (see group figure). When large it tends to push the eyes apart and outward. Sizer says: "The width between the eyes is the indication of its development. . . . When small the eyes are nearer together, which gives a pinched expression to that part of the face; when the organ is large, the eyes appear to be separated, pushing away from the root of the nose. Distinguished artists have the eyes widely separated." Audobon said of Bewick, an eminent English wood-engraver, "His eyes were placed farther apart than those of any man I have ever seen."

SIZE. This Quality manifests in a cognizance, appreciation, and recollection of the *size* and *magnitude* of objects observed. Those in whom it is large most readily perceive, recognize and remember the size, dimensions, proportion, distance, height and depth, quantity, bulk of things. It manifests outer form on each side of Observation, but a little lower down (see group figure), in the angle formed by the root of the nose and arch of the eyebrows. Prof. O. S. Fowler says: "In proportion as it is large it causes the inner portion of the eyebrows to project over the inner portions of the eyes, quite like the eaves of a house, forming a shed over the inner portion of each eye."

WEIGHT. This Quality manifests in a cognizance, appreciation, and recollection of *weight, balance and gravity* of things. Those in whom it is large most readily perceive, recognize, and remember the weight of things; and also things out of balance or plumb. These people seem to have the faculty of balancing themselves nicely, and keeping their feet on a slippery surface, on a tight-rope, etc., and often walk with a swinging, free motion, indicating a sense of balance and security. This Quality manifests under the eyebrows, next to Size, about a half inch from the upper part of the nose, rising somewhat above the inner part of the eyeball and the bridge of the nose. Prof. O. S. Fowler says: "Draw a perpendicular line from the centre of each eye up to the eyebrow; Weight is *internally*, and Color *externally* of this line under the eyebrows."

COLOR. This Quality manifests in a cognizance, appreciation, and recollection of the color, hue, shade, and tint of things. Those in whom it is large most readily perceive, recognize and remember the colors, shadings, blendings and combination of tints, and to compare, match and harmonize colors instinctively. It manifests outer form under the eyebrows, just back of Weight (see rule for finding, in last paragraph), and occupies the space directly under the centre of the arch of the eyebrows (see group figure). When largely developed it gives an upward and forward arch to the eyebrows.

ORDER. This Quality manifests in a cognizance, appreciation, and recollection of *order, method and arrangement.* Those in whom it is large most readily perceive, recognize, and remember the order and sequence in which objects appear or are arranged. They are very methodical, precise, and pay attention to details of arrangement and system. They "have a place for everything," and like to "keep everything in its place." In business they are "strong on system," sometimes overdoing it. They are also fond of rules, laws, customs, and codes, and adhere strictly thereto. They like everything pigeon-holed, labelled, or else fenced in and off from every other thing. Are also great disciplinarians. This Quality manifests outer form next to Color, and beneath the junction of the bony ridges (on the sides of the head) and the eyebrows, (see group figure). Prof. O. S. Fowler says: "When very large it forms an arch, almost an angle, in the eyebrows at this point, accompanied by its projection or hanging over. . . . When small, the eyebrows at this point retire, and are straight and flat, wanting that arched projection given by large Order." Combe says: "Its large development produces a square appearance at the external angle of the lower part of the forehead."

CALCULATION. This Quality manifests in a cognizance, appreciation, and recollection of *number, figures, calculations, etc.* Those in whom it is largely developed most readily perceive, recognize, and remember anything concerned with the *number* of things, or calculations based thereon. They are natural arithmeticians and mathematicians. Calculation comes easy to them, and in cases of high development they may be said to "think mathematically." This Quality manifests outer form next to Order, and under the outer ends of the eyebrows (see group figure).

Prof. O. S. Fowler, says: "It elongates the ends of the eyebrows laterally, and flexes them horizontally in proportion as it is developed, yet when deficient the eyebrow is left short externally, does not project beyond the eye, and terminates running *downwards.*" Gall says: "Its convolution is a continuation of the lowest convolution of Tune, and is placed on the most external part of the orbital plate, in a furrow running from before backwards. When it is very large it depresses the external part of the plate, so that the superorbital arch is irregular, except in its internal part; its external line representing a straight line, which descends obliquely. Hence the external part of the eyelid is depressed, and conceals the corresponding part of the eye."

TUNE. This Quality manifests in a cognizance, appreciation, and recollection of *tune, music, harmony, melody*, etc. Those in whom it is large most readily perceive, recognize, and remember all connected with the subject of Music. It is the musical sense, taste and faculty. Its characteristics are too well-known to require elaboration. It manifests outer form in the lateral and lower part of the forehead, above Order and Calculation, in front of Constructiveness, and back of Time (see group figure). Prof. O. S. Fowler says: "When large it fills out the lower, frontal portions of the temples. . . . Still, being located in a kind of corner . . . and the temporal muscle passing over it, its position varies somewhat, which renders observation more difficult, except in the heads of children, in whom it is generally larger than in adults."

TIME. This Quality manifests in a cognizance, appreciation, and recollection of *time, duration, rhythm, etc.* Those in whom it is large most readily perceive, recognize, and remember all connected with the flight of time, dates, duration, periodicity, chronology, etc. Spurzheim says of it that it, "perceives the duration, simultaneousness, and succession of phenomena." It may be called "the time sense" which is so apparent in some persons, and so noticeable by reason of its absence in others. It manifests outer form above Color and Weight, in front of Tune, and back of Locality (see group figure).

LOCALITY. This Quality manifests in a cognizance, appreciation, and recollection of *places, positions, locations, directions,* etc. Those in whom it is large most readily perceive, recognize, and remember places, directions, positions, land-marks, points-of-the compass, roads, paths, streets, and other things having to do with *space.* Such persons are never "lost" nor confused as to direction or locality; they have an almost instinctive "sense of direction." It is the geographical or traveller's sense. It is found large in the majority of travellers, sailors, civil engineers, etc. Persons in whom it is large can find themselves about a strange city without trouble, and will remember old scenes, places, locations for years. Those in whom it is weak frequently "get lost," or mixed up regarding place, position and direction.

It manifests outer form over Size and Weight, or about three-quarters of an inch above the inner half of the eyebrows, and runs upwards and outwards (see group figure). It is said to have been immensely developed and apparent in Capt. Cook, the eminent explorer, and the portraits of Columbus and other great explorers and travellers show a distinct enlargement of this locality. Gall, who discovered the location of this Quality, took casts of the heads of noted explorers and travellers, and others manifesting the "sense of place and direction," and upon comparing them, "found in them all, in the region directly over the eyes, two large prominences, which began just inside the root of the nose, and ascended obliquely upwards and outwards as far as the middle of the forehead." Dr. Caldwell states that, "Daniel Boone who was perpetually going from one place to another, was the most celebrated hunter and woodsman of his age, and possessed this organ in a degree of development so bold and prominent that it deformed his face."

EVENTUALITY. This Quality manifests in a cognizance appreciation and recollection of *facts, events, happenings, occurrences, news, etc.* Those in whom it is large most readily perceive, recognize and remember striking events, facts, doings, occurrences—in short, *news*. Such persons have the "nose for news" which is so important to the newspaper man, scientific investigator, researcher in any line, and general investigator. It is the "historical faculty," and the "journalistic sense," as well as an important part of the "scientific instinct." These people make good witnesses, story tellers, and entertainers. They know "what is going on," and are the people to go to when one wishes to "hear the news," or to learn the past history of anything or anybody.

This Quality manifests outer form in the centre of the forehead, immediately above Observation, and in front of Locality (see group figure). When large it tends to "fill out" the middle of the forehead. Prof. O. S. Fowler says: "It sometimes seems deficient, because the surrounding organs are large, whereas close inspection shows it to be large. Steady the head with the left hand, and place the second finger of the right in the very centre of the forehead, firmly on the head, and then work the skin horizontally. If your finger caresses an up-and-down ridge about the size of a pipe-stem, this faculty is vigorous, and has been much used and strengthened by culture of late years. Where it is not noticeably full, but has been taxed by business or literary pursuits, or had a great many little things to do for years, it appears deficient to the eye, but the rule just given for this perpendicular pipe-stem ridge signifies great activity and vigor in it." (See group figure.)

WORDS. This Quality manifests in a cognizance, appreciation and recollection of *words, terms, phrases, etc.*, and their meanings. Those in whom it is large most readily perceive, recognize and remember the words, expressions, gestures and other modes of communication between the minds of men, and are proficient not only in perceiving and understanding them, but also in employing and using them. It is the taste, power, and ability to receive verbal Impressions and to manifest verbal Expression. It produces the orator, and the adept in the use of words in writing. To those persons in whom it is largely developed, words take on life and reality, and become living thought. In excess, it produces verbosity, talkativeness, and "windiness" of expression. When deficient, it renders one unable to properly express himself. It manifests outer form above and partly behind the superorbital plates, which form the roof of the sockets of the eyes, and when large tends to press the eyes forward and downward. Its location was discovered by Gall, who observed that those fluent in the use of words almost always had *full and prominent eyes, and prominent under eye-lids.* The fullness of the eyes and lower eyelids, therefore, is its distinguishing mark.

Professor O. S. Fowler says: "See how the eyes stand out beyond the cheekbone—the best standard points from which to estimate its size, because, though it may be large, yet the Perceptives may be still larger, in which case the latter will project forward still farther even beyond large Expression.

(Words). Hence the fullness of the eyes should not be compared with the eyebrows as much as *with the bone below them*, which not being subject to kindred mutations, forms a correct measuring point of observation." The pressure outward of the under eyelids, is a good sign of the development of this Quality. It may be objected to that Quality of Words is not, strictly speaking, a *Perceptive*, but when it is realized that before words may be fluently used, they must be *perceived, recognized, and remembered*, the reason for our inclusion of this Quality in the Perceptive class may be understood.

CHAPTER XIV

THE REFLECTIVE QUALITIES

The ninth group is known as the Reflective Qualities, which is composed of the two following particular Qualities: *Analysis* and *Logic, respectively.* This group is accorded the highest place among the mental Qualities, for Reason is ranked higher than Emotion, Feeling or Sentiment. Its purpose is to philosophize, penetrate, investigate, originate, pursue the processes of inductive and deductive reasoning, analyze, synthesize, take apart, put together, combine, harmonize, search for, discover, and to manifest all the processes of Rational Thought, using the report of the Perceptives as "raw material." This group manifests outer form in the upper part of the forehead, immediately above the Reflective Qualities. (See Fig. 10.) When large it gives to the upper part of the forehead that appearance of *intellectuality,* which is so commonly recognized, and which has given rise to the semi-slang phrase "high-brow" as applied to persons manifesting intellect.

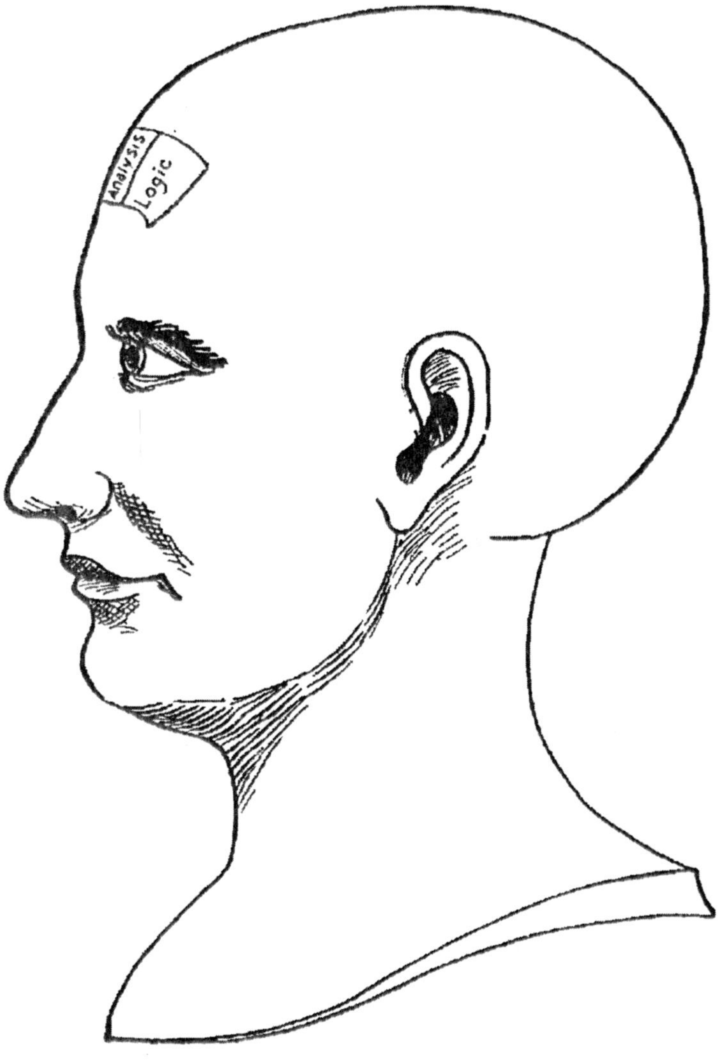

Fig. 10
THE REFLECTIVE QUALITIES

ANALYSIS. This Quality manifests in a strong desire to *analyze, compare, classify, infer, discriminate, illustrate, etc.* It gathers together the "raw material" of perception, and proceeds to analyze and compare its particular parts, and then to group the parts together in a new classification and synthesis. Those in whom it is largely developed manifest the power of *comparison* to a high degree, discovering points of resemblance and difference almost intuitively. They will plunge to the heart of a subject in a short time, and will be able to extract the *essence* of an object or subject with comparatively little effort.

Spurzheim says of it: "The great law of this faculty seems to be to form abstract ideas, generalizations, and harmony among the operations of the other faculties. . . . It pre-supposes, however, the activity of the other faculties, and cannot act upon them if they are inactive."

Professor Nelson Sizer says that it, "frequently discovers unexpected resemblances among other things, and people who have it in a very active condition are constantly surprising those in whom it is dull by their novel illustrations. It is the source of the ability some writers possess of using frequently metaphors and analogies. . . . While it contributes to reason, it is not strictly so, *per se* . . . It endeavors to prove that one thing is of such and such a nature, because it resembles another that is so and so; and because the majority of people have it fairly developed, they are prone to convert an illustration into an argument. It exercises a most important influence upon the mind in the way of analytical capability; and one who has it largely developed is quick in discovering and understanding differences, enigmatical assertions and improper or inaccurate allusions; hence it is essential to critical acumen."

Gall says, regarding its discovery: "I often conversed with a philosopher endowed with great vivacity, who, when unable to prove his point by logic, had recourse to a comparison, by which he often threw his opponents off the track, which he could not do by arguments." It tends to reason by analogy, and to make rapid and clever generalizations. The majority of scientists have it largely developed, as also do discoverers in all lines of investigation and research, and as Gall says: "Its possessors seize and judge well of the relations of things, etc., and are well fitted for business." It is attracted by investigation and thought regarding concrete things, rather than by abstract subjects. It is scientific, rather than philosophical.

As Prof. O. S. Fowler says, it: "illustrates with great cleverness and facility from the known to the unknown, and discovers the deeper analogies which pervade nature, and has an extraordinary power of discovering new truths. It reasons clearly and correctly from conclusions and scientific facts up to the laws which govern them; discerns the known from the unknown; detects error by its incongruity with facts; has an excellent talent for comparing, explaining, expounding, criticising, exposing, etc.; employs similes and metaphors well; puts this and that together, and draws correct inferences from them."

This Quality manifests in outer form in the middle of the upper part of the forehead, along the middle-line, just below the hair, directly above Eventuality, and between the two lobes of Logic (see group figure). Prof.

O. S. Fowler says of it: "It commences at the centre of the forehead and runs upward nearly to the hair. When it projects beyond surrounding organs it resembles a cone, its apex forming a ridge which widens as it rises. Its ample development elevates the middle of the upper portion of the forehead, and gives it an ascending form."

LOGIC. This Quality manifests in a strong desire to inquire into the "Why?" of things—into Causes—into the "Wherefore?"; and to reason therefrom to *effects* and application of laws. Those in whom it is large manifest the power of *logical reasoning* to a high degree, and abhor fallacies. This is the *philosophical* faculty of mind. It searches back of facts and phenomena for *causes, motives and laws,* and then reasons deductively from these. Combe says: "This faculty prompts us on all occasions to ask, "Why is this so, and what is its object?" It *demands reasons and proofs* in the reasoning of its owner, as well as from others."

Prof. Nelson Sizer says: "It gives ability to look deeply into subjects, and to appreciate the logical sequences of arguments, hence it is large in persons who indicate genius in metaphysics, political economy, and all sciences of a profound character. . . . When prominent, and the perceptive faculties are moderate, and Comparison (Analysis) is not equally influential, it tends to speculative thinking. Men so constituted are given to spinning improbable theories; their notions are too abstract for ordinary minds, and they are looked upon as dull and heavy weights in society. On the other hand when it (Logic) is deficient, the individual is superficial and incapable of taking comprehensive views of subjects; or forming judgments that will apply to the affairs of life successfully.

Professor O. S. Fowler says that this Quality gives "the desire to know the *why and wherefore* of things, and to investigate their laws; ability to reason from causes down to effects, and from effects up to causes; the therefore and wherefore; ability to adapt ways and means to ends, to plan, contrive, invent, create resources, apply power advantageously, make heads save hands, kill two birds with one stone, predict the results of given measures, etc."

This Quality manifests outer form in the sides of the upper part of the forehead, one either side of Analysis and over Locality (see group figure). When large it gives to the forehead a "high, bold, square" form. With large Perceptives this Quality does not present so prominent an appearance and so marked a comparison, but with the Perceptives small it gives to the brow an "overhanging" appearance. With Analysis equally, or nearly as strong, the fullness of course extends well across the forehead; but with Analysis much smaller, Logic presents a bulging on each side of the forehead; while with Analysis large and Logic small, the latter gives the appearance of two depressions on each side of the forehead.

Spurzheim well says of the combination of Analysis and Logic (which he terms "Comparison" and "Causality," respectively): "Causality and Comparison combined constitute Reason. Without Causality (Logic) there can be no argumentative reasoning; without Comparison (Analysis), no comprehensive views, and no nice distinctions. Observation teaches objects, and Eventuality facts, while Comparison (Analysis) points out their identity, analogy, difference or harmony, whereas Causality (Logic) seeks their causes, and all together discern general principles and laws; draw conclusions, inductions and creations, and constitute a truly philosophical understanding."

CHAPTER XV

THE RELIGIO-MORAL QUALITIES

The tenth group is known as the Religio-Moral Qualities, and is composed of the following particular Qualities: *Reverence, Mysticism, Optimism,* and *Conscientiousness,* respectively. This group manifests outer form at the front-top of the head, and on either side thereof (see Fig. 11).

REVERENCE. This Quality manifests in a strong reverence, respect and awe for and of higher beings, persons in authority, sacred things, religious ideas, constituted authority, leaders, teachers, and heroes. It may be symbolically expressed by the word, "Worship." Like that of Mysticism, this Quality contains within its field the highest and the lowest. It manifests the reverence and veneration for the highest conceptions of Deity and Being; and also the fear and base servile worship of idols, demoniac deities, devil-gods, etc. Likewise, it manifests in respect and submission for the lawfully constituted authorities; and also for false leaders and prophets, charla-

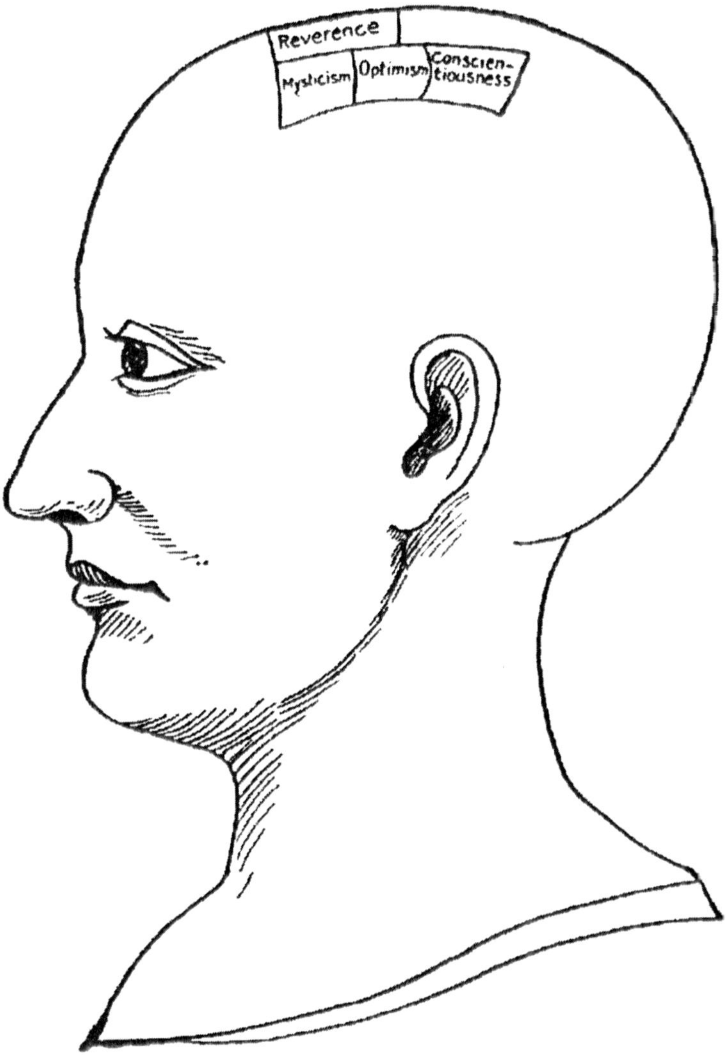

Fig. 11
THE RELIGIO-MORAL QUALITIES

tans and imposters. In the same way it causes a hero-worship for those who have performed meritorious tasks and have wrought good for the race; but also for the unworthy persons whose sensational deeds have brought them into the "limelight" of notoriety. It manifests in all forms of the highest religion; and in the lowest forms of devil-worship and low superstitious awe and fear, in the richest religious experiences, and in the wildest fanaticism and hallucinations. The direction of the manifestation is decided by the relative development of the other propensities, particularly those of the reasoning faculties.

This Quality manifests outer form on the middle-top of the head, along the middle-line directly in front of Firmness, back of Sympathy, and just above Mysticism and Optimism (see group figure). When largely developed, it causes the middle of the top of the head to "bulge," particularly if Mysticism be also largely developed, the combination usually being thus.

MYSTICISM. This Quality manifests in a strong attraction for the supernatural, the marvellous, the unknown, the mysterious.

When perverted it leads to superstition, gross credulity, belief in witchcraft; faith in signs, omens, and warnings, etc. When balanced by certain other Qualities it leads one to the higher flights of religious experience, faith, and consciousness of the "light within;" but when not so balanced it leads one to credulity, superstition and religious, occult, and mystical imposture.

"Psychic" phenomena are familiar to those in whom it is largely developed in connection with certain other mental qualities; clairvoyance, second-sight, spirit-vision and other peculiar experiences being common to these people. The prophets, seers, and wonder-workers belong to this class of "psychics." Poets possess this Quality in many cases. The manifestations of this Quality include some of the very highest and the very lowest of "spiritual" experiences and feelings. This paradox is explained when we consider the influence of the other Qualities, high and low, operating in connection with that of Mysticism. In the garden of Mysticism grow the choicest flowers and the rankest and most noxious weeds.

This Quality is located immediately in front of Optimism, and below on either side of Reverence, on the front-upper part of the head (see group figure). When developed it renders the front top-head broad and prominent.

OPTIMISM. This Quality manifests in a strong tendency to look on the bright side of things, to expect the best, to anticipate the best. Spurzheim says of it: "Hope is necessary to the happiness of man in almost all situations and often gives more satisfaction than even success. Those who are everlastingly scheming or building castles in the air have it large. It believes possible whatever the other faculties desire. It is not confined to this life, but inspires hopes of a future state, and belief in the immortality of the soul. When too strong it expects the unreasonable and impossible; but when too weak, with Caution large, it produces low spirits, melancholy and despair."

This Quality when full produces optimists; when weak, pessimists; when medium, the average person who swings between the two extremes partaking of the nature of each.

Those in whom it is developed to excess are apt to see success in everything, and with a lively imagination translate dreams into realities; of these persons it has been said: "show them an egg, and the next minute the air is full of feathers." When this Quality is weak the person is disposed to look for the worm in the apple, decay at the heart of the rose, and for the skeleton beneath the form of beauty. It has been said that "the optimist sees nothing but the body of the doughnut; the pessimist, nothing but the hole."

This Propensity manifests outer form at the middle sides of the upper head, in front of Conscientiousness, back of Spirituality (see group figure).

CONSCIENTIOUSNESS. This Quality manifests in a strong tendency to act according to truth, principle, duty, the accepted code of ethics, conception of right, accepted religious teachings—in short to regulate conduct according to the particular standard of "right and wrong" accepted by the person. Those in whom it is large feel keenly their personal responsibility, duty, and moral obligation. With Reverence large, they model their standard of duty upon religious standards, while with Reverence small, and Sociability large, they model their standard upon social ethics, the Brotherhood of Man, and the "social conscience." In fact the Quality itself gives rise to what is generally called the "social conscience."

Combe says of this Propensity: "After more than thirty years experience of the world in actual life, and in various countries, I cannot remember an instance in which I have been permanently treated unjustly by one in whom this organ and intellect were large. Momentary injustice, through irritation or misrepresentation, may have been done; but after correct information and time to become cool, I have found such persons ever disposed to act on the dictates of Conscience; as well satisfied with justice. . . . It leads to punctuality in keeping appointments so as not to waste their time; to the ready payment of debts; will not send collectors away unsatisfied except from inability to pay; are reserved in making promises, but punctual in keeping them; and when favorably combined, are consistent in conduct. . . . Its predominance makes a strict disciplinarian and a rigid but just master; invests all actions with a sense of duty; thereby sometimes rendering estimable persons disagreeable."

In normal manifestation this Quality renders its possessor a most worthy and estimable individual; but when abnormally developed and not balanced by judgment and the reasoning faculties, it produces persecutors and religious and ethical tyrants, adhering to the letter of the law rather than to its spirit. Conscience is generally esteemed, but careful observers deplore the "ingrown conscience" and "blue-law spirit" of those of large Conscientiousness, large Destructiveness, and small Sympathy. Many so-called "reformers" belong to this last class. This Quality manifests outer form on the side of the top part of the head, just below and on either side of Firmness. It lies between Firmness and Cautiousness, with Optimism just in front of it and Approbativeness just back of it (see group figure).

CHAPTER XVI

FACES

Next to the shape of the head, the facial expression furnishes us with the most marked indication of the outer form accompanying the inner mental state. In fact, many authorities hold that the facial expression affords the most easily read and most comprehensive index of character, and that, therefore, Physiognomy possesses many points of superiority over Phrenology. The truth seems to be that Physiognomy and Phrenology are twin-sciences, and that the true student of Human Nature should acquaint himself thoroughly with both.

Physiognomy is "the science and art of discovering or reading the temper and other characteristic qualities of the mind by the features of the face." The philosophy underlying the science of Physiognomy has been stated at length in the first several chapters of this book, the essence of which is that *mental states manifest in outward form.* The majority of persons apply the principles of

Physiognomy more or less unconsciously in judging the characters of those with whom they come in contact. Nearly every one scans closely the features of those whom they meet for the first time, and form a general impression therefrom. Children and domestic animals possess an instinctive knowledge of facial expression and can often tell very accurately the general disposition toward them possessed by various persons. Certain persons are generally considered to "look stupid," while others have "a bright, intelligent expression"; some look "tricky," while others "look honest" and trustworthy.

Professor Nelson Sizer says: "Though all human beings have the general human form and features—though all have eyes, nose, mouth, chin, etc., yet each one has a different face and look from every other. And, more, yet, the same person has a very different facial look at different times, according as he is angry or friendly, etc. And always the same look when in the same mood. Of course, then, something causes this expression—especially, since all who are angry, friendly, etc., have one general or similar expression; that is, one look expresses anger, another affection, another devotion, another kindness, etc. And since nature always works by means, she must needs have her physiognomical tools. Nor are they under the control of the will, for they act spontaneously. We cannot help, whether we will or no, laughing when merry, even though in church, pouting when provoked, and expressing all our mental operations, down even to the very innermost recesses of our souls, in and by our countenances. And with more minuteness and completeness than by words, especially when the expressions are intense or peculiar."

Professor Drayton says. "Everything, from head to feet, of form, size, and action, indicates in some degree, the character of the individual, or state of mind, and feeling in exercise for the time being. The arching or depressing of the eyebrows, the full opening or partial closing of the eye, the pursing or pouting of the lips, the firm set jaw, the elevated head, the lofty shoulders, the stiff attitude, the dignified and stately step, or the reverse of this, will impress each observer in respect to the changing moods which may exist in a given individual. . . . Each of the mental organs has its natural language, as shown in pantomine, which is exhibited by the gestures and motions of the head, hands and body. Children and animals read the feelings of their parents or masters by their motions and attitudes, which are often more influential than words. The brain is the central source of motive and mental power; every action has its root or seat of impulse in the brain and its connections, and as the mind forms purposes, the will is sent out to the extremities, and the external motions express the inward thought and feeling. Habitual states of mind tend to produce habitual forms and expressions of face and body; a person who suffers pain for years, will have in the face an expression of the internal state; one who has been nurtured in gladness, though the face may not be beautiful, will wear the sunshine of joy; one who has had care and responsibility, will come to show it in the face, in the walk, and in the voice, as one who has been subjugated and kept subordinate will have the word humiliation written in his features not only, but in all his movements and attitudes."

SHAPES OF FACES

The authorities in Physiognomy divide the faces of persons into three general classes, viz: (1) The Round Face; (2) The Oblong Face; and (3) The Pear-shaped Face.

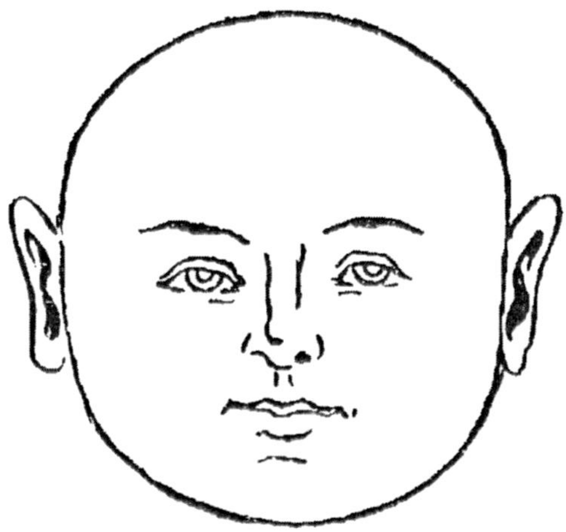

FIG. 12
ROUND FACE

In Fig. 12, we see the Round Face. This face is indicative of the Vital Temperament. It is usually associated with broad shoulders, short neck, full chest, and plumpness, with enlarged abdomen in middle life. These people love ease and physical comforts, good eating and drinking, and not too much hard mental or physical work. They are solicitous of the comfort of their bodies, and generally "look out for No. 1" in this respect. They are generally good-natured and sociable, and often jolly.

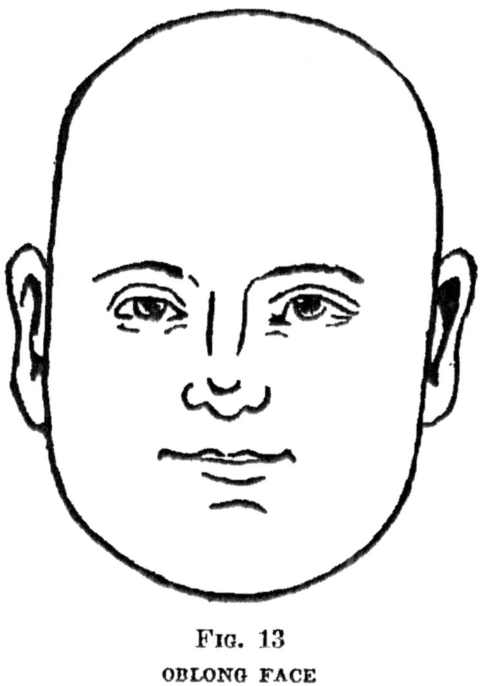

FIG. 13
OBLONG FACE

In Fig. 13, we see the Oblong Face. This face is indicative of the Motive Temperament. It is usually associated with a compact firm body, which while well filled out can scarcely be called plump, certainly not fleshy. These people are generally strong and active, persevering and sparing neither themselves or

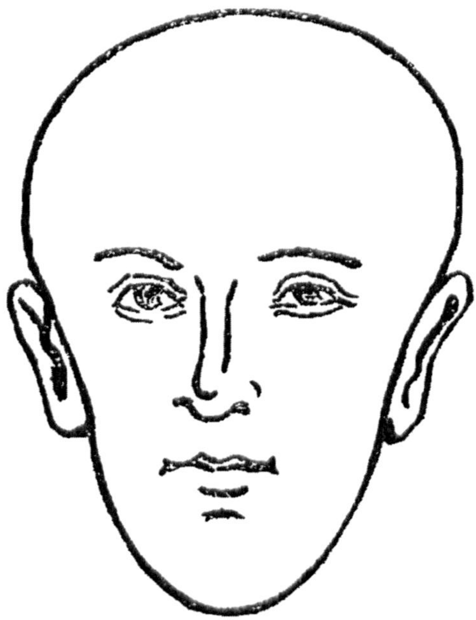

FIG. 14
PEAR-SHAPED FACE

others in the direction of work. They are apt to have a very fair share of common sense; are *practical;* and are generally *reliable.*

In Fig. 14, we see the Pear-shaped Face. This face is indicative of the Mental Temperament. It is usually associated with a delicately formed body, and finely proportioned physical shape; the shoulders often being narrow, and the neck long. These people manifest the characteristics of mental and nervous force, rather than of vital or motive energy. They often have bright, expressive eyes, and show other signs of the artistic or literary character. They are inclined to be sensitive and impressionable, and to suffer and enjoy keenly.

In addition to the aforementioned general types, there are several others which are modifications thereof, and which we shall now consider.

In Fig. 15, we see the Square Face. This face indicates a combination of the Motive and Vital Temperaments, with the Religio-Moral Qualities deficient and the Selfish-Qualities predominant. These people usually have square, stocky bodies, strong and wiry, and are tenacious of life. They are Materialistic to a degree, and cannot understand others who differ temperamentally from them. Usually, they have Combativeness and Destructiveness large; strong Perceptive

Qualities; and but moderate Conscientiousness. They look out for themselves, pushing others aside, and not being disturbed by "the higher feelings." They are generally stub-

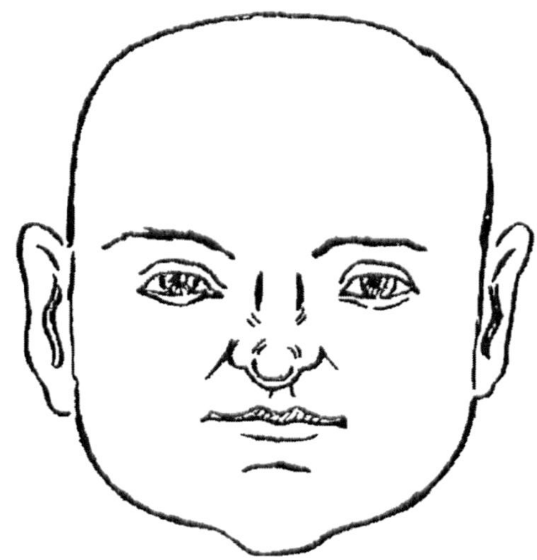

FIG. 15
SQUARE FACE

born; and their weak point is apt to be Amativeness.

In Fig. 16, we see the Egg-shaped Face. This face indicates the Mental Temperament with the Psychic Qualities largely in the ascendent. The Selfish Qualities are weak, while the Qualities of Mysticism, Reverence and Ideality are large. These people are generally known as "spiritual," and are often very "psychic." They are generally imprac-

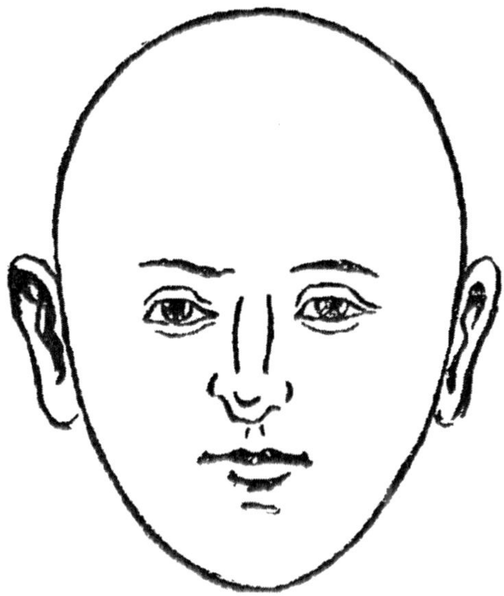

FIG. 16
EGG-SHAPED FACE

tical and dwell in an ideal world apart from the things of earth.

In Fig. 17, we see the Inverted-Egg-shaped Face. This face indicates the extreme form of the Vital Temperament, associated with an absence of the active qualities which should accompany it. The Mental and Motive

Qualities are quite deficient, while the purely *Animal* Qualities are strong. The result is a *pig-like* nature, content with wallowing in the mud of the animal propensities and hav-

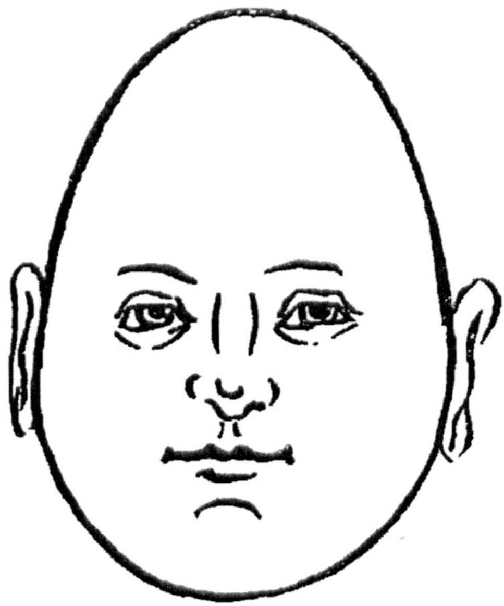

FIG. 17
INVERTED EGG-SHAPED FACE

ing a full swill-barrel. These people are essentially lazy, gross, worthless, and animal-like. Note the large lower-face (without the strong jaw), and the small upper head. Note the broad nose, and general lazy expression.

In Figs. 18 and 19, respectively, we see

the contrast between Broad and Narrow Faces. The rule is that Broad Faces indicate fight, destructiveness, and acquisitiveness—the Selfish Faculties, in fact; while Narrow

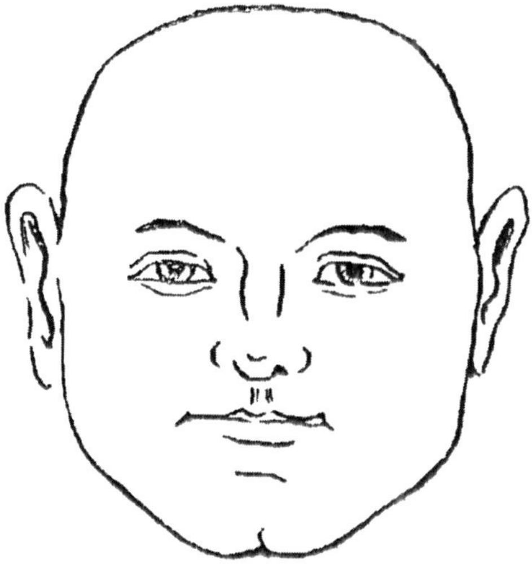

FIG. 18
BROAD FACE

Faces indicate a lack of these qualities. The broad-headed animals are the fighters, while the narrow-heads are the timid and peaceful, as a rule. The same principle applies in the case of men. Look over the charts of the Qualities, and see why this is.

The above mentioned several types or

classes of faces have, of course, innumerable variations and combinations, but a careful study of these several types will give one the general key to all faces. It is well to obtain a

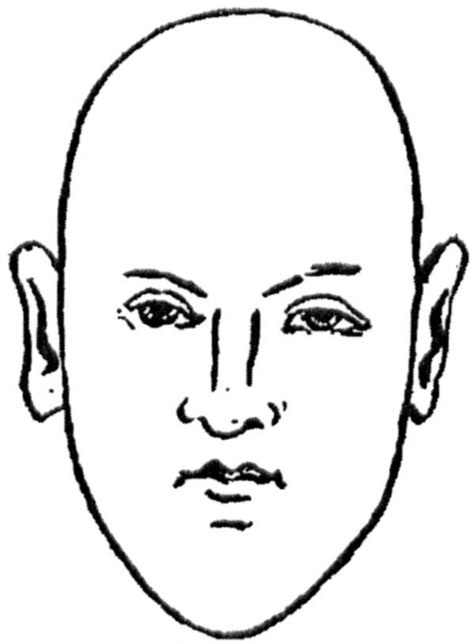

FIG. 19
NARROW FACE

side view, as well as a full-face view, of the face one wishes to study.

In studying faces, not only the general shape of the face must be observed, but also the various features thereof, as for instance: the chin; the mouth; the nose; the eyes; the ears; etc. These features form the subject of the following chapters.

CHAPTER XVII

CHINS AND MOUTHS

Physiognomists regard the chin as an important feature to be considered in the study of faces as the outer form of character. The following are the principal points of the "reading" of chins.

In Fig. 20 we see the first point to be observed in the study of chins. The rule is to draw an imaginary perpendicular line from the point at the root of the nose, between the two eyebrows. In the normal and average type, the line touches the upper lip and chin. But we find the normal condition in but comparatively few cases, the majority manifesting a variation backward or forward. When the chin is found to recede from the line, it is interpreted as an indication of weakness, lack of stability and firmness, and a general vacillating and unstable character. When the chin projects beyond the line, it is interpreted as indicating firmness, stubborness, and a generally selfish nature, which is considered "strong" by contrast with the "weak" receding chin. When the projecting chin is *pointed,* it indicates that the strength is manifested as grasping, miserliness, etc.; while if it is *square,* it indicates Combativeness and

FIG. 20
CHIN STUDY

Destructiveness as well as Acquisitiveness; and if it is *very broad and square,* it indicates the domineering, "bossy," tyrannical, self-willed character.

The above points regarding the chin must always be taken into consideration. The following points are based on the shape of the chin when in *normal position,* that is when the perpendicular line descends in a straight line from the root of the nose to the chin:

The *narrow-round chin* indicates *idealistic feeling* not manifesting in decided action. These people have high desires, longings, and aspiration, but lack the will to act upon the same.

The *narrow-square chin* indicates the idealistic nature, *accompanied by the will to act* upon the same.

The *broad-round chin* indicates *substantial feeling,* without the will to manifest it in decided action. These people desire ordinary, plain, practical things, but lack the initiative, will and nerve to overcome obstacles to acquire them.

The broad-square chin indicates that the feelings are plain, practical and substantial, *with the will to back them up.*

From the above, it will be seen that *roundness* indicates *feeling;* and that *squareness* denotes *will;* that *narrowness* denotes *ideal-*

ity; while *broadness* denotes *practical, substantial, plain* desires and tastes.

The dimpled or indented chin indicates the warm artistic temperament with its accompanying desire for love of the opposite sex, desire for affection, and alas! too often a fickleness and lack of loyalty and fidelity in love affairs.

JAWS

A *broad, firm jaw* indicates strong Combativeness, Destructiveness and Firmness.

A *narrow, loose jaw* indicates the reverse of the qualities above noted.

A *loose, drooping jaw and open mouth* indicates timidity, weakness, shyness, or despondency.

The *fighters* in all walks of life manifest the strong, firm jaw. It is the survival of the primitive "bite" in the animal or cave-man.

MOUTHS

The Orientals have a proverb which runs as follows: "By a man's eyes, know what he might have been, or may be; by his mouth, knew what he has been, and is." The study of the mouth is one of the greatest interest, and one which will richly repay one for his time and thought. It will be noticed that there is a great difference between the mouth and lips of an individual in childhood, in youth, and in middle-age, which fact shows the truth of the Oriental proverb just quoted. The mouth indeed shows what a man has been and is.

Small mouths generally denote undeveloped, childish, or babyish character, neither good nor bad.

Large mouths denote matured character, good or bad. When firm, they denote force and energy. When half-open, they denote dullness and heaviness. When showing full protruding lips, they denote sensuality and selfish passions and tastes. When very large and flexible, they denote the "windy" person who is fond of talking and hearing the sound of his own voice—when one says that another is "big-mouthed" he states a truth which physiognomy bears out.

An *upward curve* of the corners of the mouth, denotes a cheerful, optimistic disposition and mental attitude. Likewise, a *downward curve* denotes a despondent, pessimistic disposition and mental attitude. A graceful bow-like curve, shows a well-balanced and "all around" disposition.

Tightly closed lips indicate a firmness, and often a "closeness" of disposition. *Loosely closed lips* indicate a lack of firmness, and often a spendthrift tendency. *Lips that touch lightly and protrude slightly* in a "kiss-like" shape, indicate vanity, love of praise and flattery, and often a desire to be petted.

Puffed-out lips indicate sloth, dullness, lack of energy and ambition, general heaviness. *Coarse lips* indicate lack of refinement, and often grossness. *Particularly full lips* indicate Amativeness and sometimes Sensuality.

Slanting mouths indicate trickiness, "foxiness" and general unreliability. *Crooked mouths*, or mouths greatly out of symmetry, are held by many authorities to indicate lack of Conscientiousness, and often criminal tendencies.

Full, red, middle-lips indicate love of the opposite sex. *Thin, pale middle-lips* denote the opposite traits.

A long upper-lip indicates Self-Esteem. *A*

short upper-lip denotes deficient Self-Esteem, but often also a strong Approbativeness. (John D. Rockefeller has an almost abnormally long upper lip.)

The affectionate faculties are believed to manifest in outer form in the center of the lips, because of certain nerve centers at that place. A fullness and enlargement there denotes strong affection, while deficiency in the affectionate qualities manifest in the opposite direction.

Will and self-control is shown by the relative firmness and "set" of the lips and mouth.

Besides the above mentioned characteristics, the student will soon perceive that there are certain "expressions" of the lips and mouth which, although impossible of expression in words, nevertheless may be almost instinctively recognized by the careful observer. Lips, like eyes, tell their story plainly to the careful and practiced observer. It is a safe rule to *avoid those whose mouths arouse an instinctive distrust in your mind.* Watch closely the mouths of people speaking to you, and you will receive many a plain signal of danger, and many an assurance of safety. The eyes, while full of information, often deceive those not fully versed in their secret code—but the mouth tells its tale in plain, simple, understandable terms, signs and symbols.

CHAPTER XVIII

EYES, EARS AND NOSES

It has been said that "the eyes are the windows of the soul," and indeed they do express a *something* that is not possible to any other part of the face or body. When unrestrained the eye correctly portrays the innermost feelings and emotions affecting and influencing us, and in many cases we are able to get a clear and unobstructed view of the soul behind the eyes by gazing into them. But, alas! it is possible to mask the expression of the eyes, and to counterfeit emotions and feelings which do not exist within the mind. Men and women trained in the arts of dissimulation and concealment, may, and do, conceal their thoughts and feelings which ordinarily would be reflected in their eyes; and many, especially women, are able to counterfeit feelings which have no real existence in their minds or souls. We have seen women bestowing upon the unsuspecting "mere man," the most artless, ingenuous "baby stare," while at the same time their minds were filled with craft and cunning. We have seen others whose eyes portrayed the most absolute innocence and truth, while their hearts were filled with selfish, base feelings, and their minds with cunning schemes. The trained diplomat and skilled gambler successfully mask their thoughts, and their eyes reflect nothing of their secrets; and, upon occasion, they are able to throw into their eyes any desired expression. The best authorities on Physiognomy hold that the mouth is a much more reliable index of thought and character than the eye—for the eye may lie, while the mouth betrays itself even when attempting the counterfeit.

But, nevertheless, the eyes *do* betray character, not by their expression but by their shape and form. Habitual mental states reflect in the outer form of the eyes, in spite of the care of their owners not to let them tell the secret of the thought and feeling of the moment. The story is told *not by the expression* of the eye, but by the muscles surrounding the eyes, the eye-lids, etc. In fact, the *eye-lids* supply the greater part of that which we call the "expression of the eye," their contractions and relaxations producing the effect.

Secretiveness, cunning, and closeness are denoted by closely drawn eye-lids, a furtive look often being imparted thereby . This position of the eye-lids has been likened to an instinctive inclination to draw the eye-lids together to hide the expression of the eye, but it probably arises from the original trait of the animal to protect his eyes from attack when engaging in a fight, or raid. As an instance of this, it will be found that a feeling of cruelty, or desire to hurt another, will manifest in a compression of the eye-lids, and a tightening of the upper eyelid which assumes a straight form. *Frankness, truthfulness and honesty* are, in the same way, indicated by open, free looking eyes. This expression may be counterfeited upon occasions, but the counterfeit may be detected by observing the eyes when the owner is off guard.

The *fighting, destructive, motive feelings* are indicated by *straight lines* of the lids. *Affection, benevolence, sympathy, and love,* manifest in curving, drooping, full eye-lids, the absence of straight lines being marked. *Amativeness and Alimentiveness* show in very thick eye-lids, giving a sensual gross expression to the eyes. *Destructiveness* manifests in a tightening of the upper lid, and a bearing down upon the eyeball. *Approbativeness* gives a peculiar "coquettish" relaxation of the upper eye-lid, which is suggestive of the desire to wink in a meaning manner. *Humor* gives a peculiar contraction to the eye-lids, and at the same time producing the little lines radiating from each outer corner of the eye-lids—the "laughing wrinkles." *Ideality, Optimism, and Mysticism* impart an open expression to the eyes. *Cautiousness,* when large, also gives to the eyes an open, almost startled, surprised expression.

Large, protruding eyes are held to be indicative of wordiness, talkativeness, and lack of careful thought—the desire to talk for the pleasure of hearing oneself talk.

In connection with the subject of the outer form manifesting in the eyes, we would call your attention to the quotation from Prof. O. S. Fowler, appearing in Lesson XIII, in which he speaks of certain of the Perceptive Qualities which indicate in outer form in the region of the eye, as follows: "The shape of the eyebrows reveals the size, absolute and relative, of each, thus: When *all* are large, the eyebrow is long and arching; when all are deficient, it is long and straight; when some are large and others small, it arches over the large ones, but passes horizontally over those which are small. This rule is infallible." In connection therewith, we suggest that the student re-read carefully Chapter XIII, which deals with the Perceptive Qualities which manifest outer form in the region of the eye.

EARS

Many physiognomists pass lightly over the subject of the ears as an index of character, while others seem to specialize on this feature.

The *round ear* is held to indicate the Vital Temperament. The *oblong ear,* the Motive Temperament; and the *pear-shaped ear* the Mental Temperament.

Quality is held to be indicated by the relative delicateness in the moulding of the ear, a coarse, misshapen ear being held to indicate an uncultivated nature; while a delicately moulded, shapely ear is held to indicate culture and refinement.

A *long, narrow ear* is held to indicate an

ambitious, striving nature. An ear *pointed at the tip* (upper part) is held to be indicative of selfishness and general "foxiness."

NOSES

All physiognomists agree upon the importance of the nose as an index of character. The

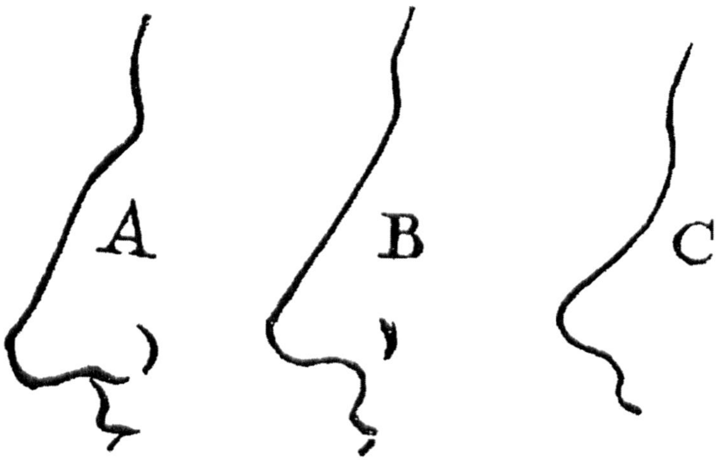

FIG. 21
A, ROMAN; B, GRECIAN; C, CHERUBIC

majority of people recognize the sign of a large, strong nose, on the one hand, and a small, weak nose on the other.

In Fig. 21 we see the three general forms of the nose, the Roman; Grecian and Cherubic; respectively. The *Roman nose* is held to be indicative of Self-Esteem, Combativeness, Destructiveness and Acquisitiveness. The *Grecian nose* is held to be indicative of Ideality, Conscientiousness, Reverence and other "higher qualities." The *Cherubic nose* is held to be indicative of feminine qualities, social attractiveness, and emotional qualities.

FIG. 22

THREE TEMPERAMENTS

There are of course innumerable modifications and combinations of these three general classes.

In Fig. 22 we see the classification adopted by some authorities, who divide the nose into three general parts, each of which is held to indicate one of the three Temperaments, and the Qualities which are related to each. Thus the hard bony part, including the bridge, indicates the Motive; the tip and end, the Mental; and the "wings" on each side of the nostrils, the Vital. There is much truth in this classification, and a careful study of this illustration will aid the student in his understanding of noses as an outer sign of character. In fact, this illustration may be used as a basis for the whole subject of the meaning of noses as outer signs of character.

Large nostrils indicate strong Vitativeness and physical well-being, and often strong Emotive Qualities. Narrow, small, or tight nostrils indicate weak Vitativeness and Vital Force An authority says: "If the nostrils are wide-apart, the man is merciful. If the nostrils are wide-open, like those of a bull, resemblances to that animal prevail in violent wrath and hard breathing."

The tip of the nose indicates the several mental qualities. The sharp pointed tip indicates an inquisitive, prying, investigating nature—a general "sharpness" so to speak. A blunt tip indicates a lack of "sharpness" and inquisitiveness. The upturned tip, or "pug," indicates a trifling, superficial, gossiping tendency. As a general rule the sharp tip indicates thought, while the rounded trip indicates feeling.

The bony part of the nose, when prominent, indicates the strength of the Motive Qualities, such as Combativeness, Destructiveness, Acquisitiveness, Constructiveness, etc. It generally accompanies the people who push forward and "do things" in spite of obstacles—it is the nose of the great generals, and the majority of great financiers.

CHAPTER XIX

MISCELLANEOUS SIGNS

While the subject of hands may be thought to belong to the study of Palmistry, with which we have no concern in this book, nevertheless we think that we should include herein a brief reference to the several classes of the hand as indicative of the outer form of mental states. That the shape of the hand often reveals information regarding the character of its owner is admitted by the best authorities on the subject. Many persons who discard the theories of Palmistry still regard the subject of the shape and meaning of hands as apart from that study, and believe that an understanding of the indications of the several classes of hands is important to the students of Human Nature.

There are seven general types of hands, viz: (1) The Spatulate; (2) the Square; (3) the Artistic; (4) the Elementary; (5) the Mixed; (6) the Philosophic; and (7) the Psychic. Following we give a brief recital of the qualities held to be indicated by each.

In Fig. 23, we see the Spatulate Hand, the special peculiarities of which are the straight, smooth fingers and the "splay" tips. This type of hand is held to indicate an

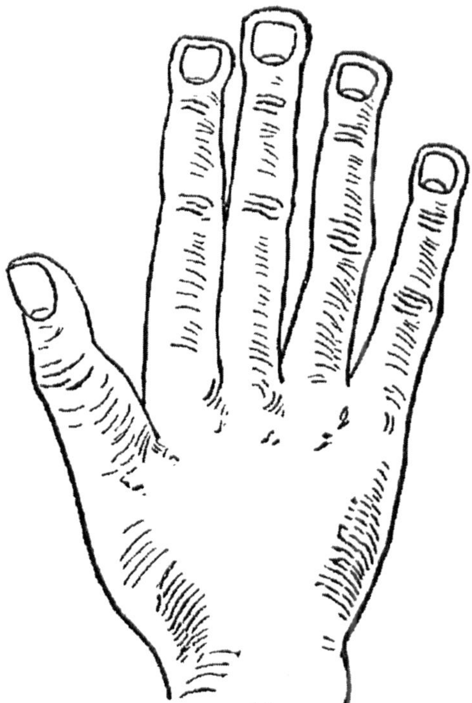

FIG. 23
SPATULATE HAND

active, energetic nature, that is satisfied only when it is employed and doing something useful. This hand is eminently "practical," and its owner cares very little for art, poetry, or literature.

In Fig. 24, we see the Square Hand, the special peculiarities of which are its general "squareness" of the palm, and generally of the finger-tips. This also is a

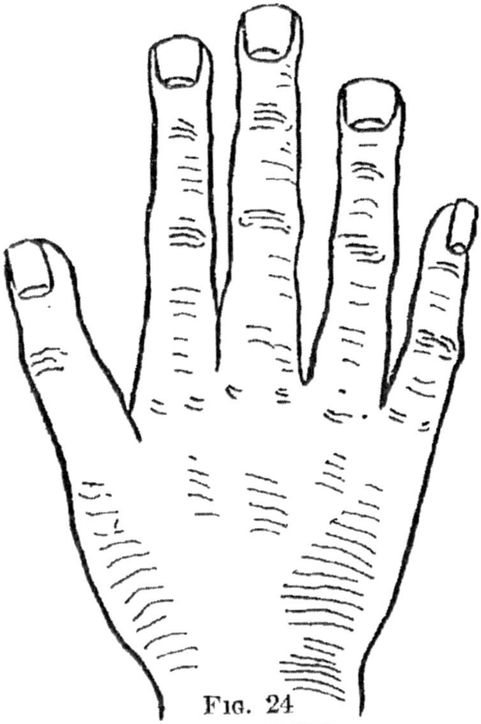

FIG. 24
SQUARE HAND

useful hand, and its owner is amenable to authority, and makes a good employee or helper. It indicates a quiet, peaceable disposition, and its owner is usually found to be careful, orderly, and dependable—the sense of *order* being especially strong.

In Fig. 25, we see the Artistic Hand, the special peculiarities of which are the suppleness and softness of the hand; its symmetrical form; and its long, tapering fingers. Its owners are of the poetic and ar-

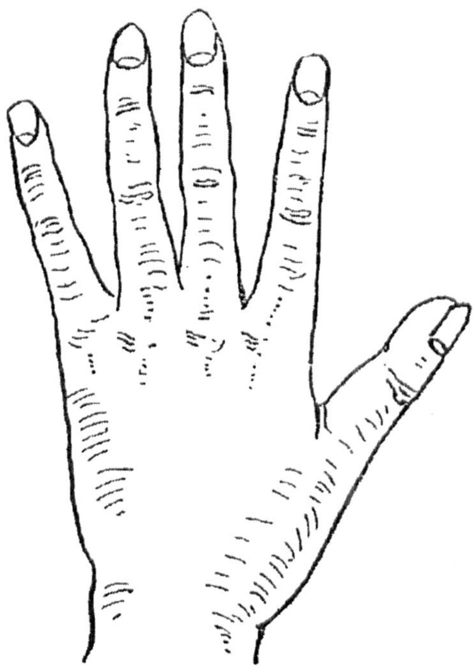

FIG. 25
ARTISTIC HAND

tistic nature, with a taste for beautiful and refined things, artistic environment, bright and witty speech, and "choice" things generally. The Qualities of Ideality and Words are apt to be well developed in these cases, and "the artistic temperament" is found in its full development here.

In Fig. 26, we see the Elementary Hand,

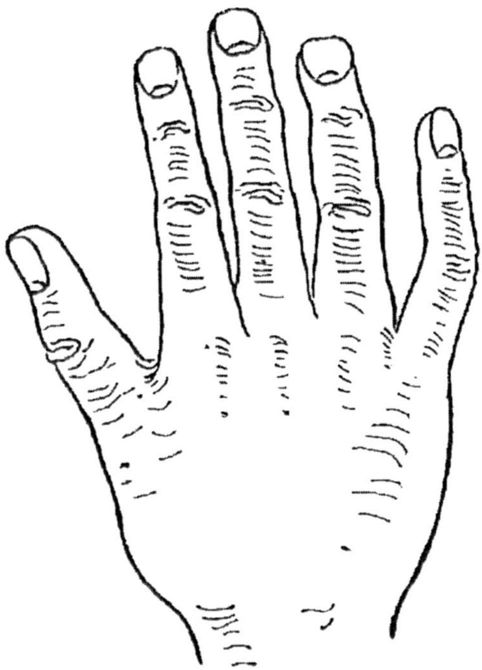

FIG. 26
ELEMENTARY HAND

the special peculiarities of which are its short, thick fingers, and its thick heavy palm. Its owners are "of the earth, earthy," and have but very little imagination and fine taste.

In Fig. 27, we have the Philosophic Hand, the special peculiarities of which are its large thumb, rounded finger-tips, and

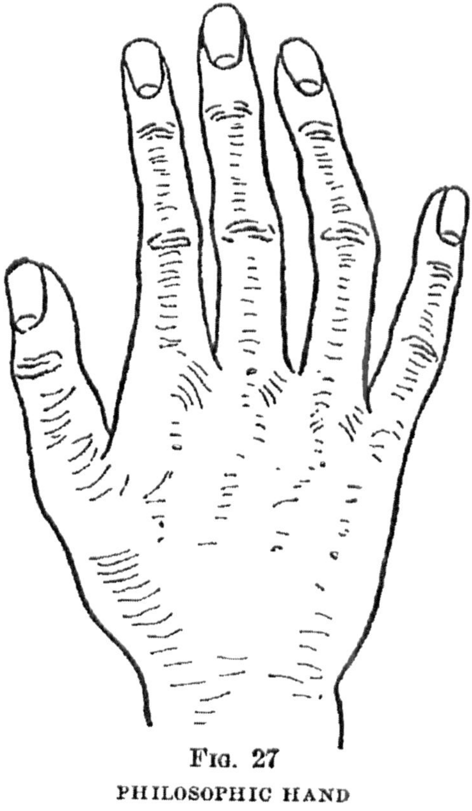

FIG. 27
PHILOSOPHIC HAND

its projecting joints. Its owners are thinkers, investigators, and reasoners along practical lines, and are generally skeptical and inclined to demand proof of anything and everything.

In Fig. 28, we see the Psychic Hand, the special peculiarities of which are the extreme slenderness of the entire hand,

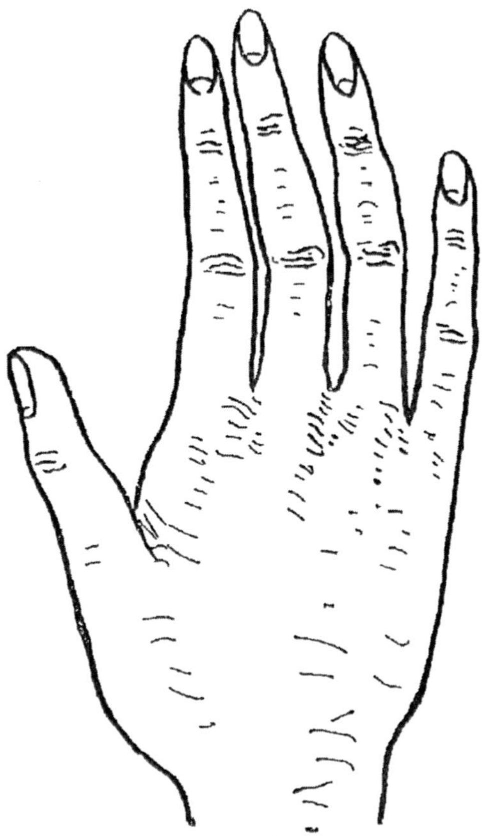

FIG. 28
PSYCHIC HAND

and the long thin, pointed fingers. Its owners have Mysticism highly developed, and incline toward the mysterious, supernatural, occult, and imaginative, and are generally of an extremely nervous, sensitive nature.

Very few hands adhere strictly to any one of these several types, but are more or less composite or "mixed." In such cases the characteristics of each type mingle and blend, and must be interpreted accordingly. The following peculiarities are also noted by the authorities:

THE THUMB. The thumb is divided into three parts, each indicating a certain quality, as follows: (1) the top part or division, which indicates Will; (2) the second or middle part, which indicates Logic; (3) the "ball" or fat lower portion, which indicates Passion. The comparative size of either of these parts indicates the strength of its particular qualities.

THE FINGERS. Hard fingers indicate work, activity, and energy. Soft fingers indicate love of ease, disinclination for work, laziness. Very hard hands denote heaviness and general stupidity, also gross tastes and undeveloped nature. Smooth fingers denote artistic tastes, etc.; while knotted fingers denote philosophic thought and argument, orderliness and taste for material facts and things. Short fingers denote quick judgment and impatience of detail; while long fingers denote a love of detail, elaboration and "fussiness." Spatulate fingers indicate tidiness, usefulness, and a desire to be doing useful work.

THE PALM. Hardness of the palm, as of the fingers, denotes activity, energy and work; while softness denotes love of ease, laziness, etc. Wideness of the palm denotes generosity, broad-mindedness, etc.; while a narrow palm denotes the reverse. Firm palms generally denote the Motive Temperament; while soft, flabby palms denote the Vital temperament.

THE WALK

The study of the Walk as an index of character is favored by many authorities. There are three general types of walks, viz (1) the long stride, in regular time; (2) the short, quick, and somewhat jerky step; (3) the short but regular step.

Those who walk with a long stride generally take a broad view of things, but if their walk is also slow they are apt to lack energy and push. The short, quick step denotes activity, but small ideas and often pettiness. The combination of the long stride and the quick movement is held to indicate both large ideas and activity. A draggy, shuffling walk is held to indicate a careless, shiftless nature; and a springy movement is indicative of mental activity. A mincing walk is held to denote "finickiness," affectation, and general artificiality; while a careless walk denotes a disregard for appearances and a general unconventional nature. Those who walk in a straight line, direct to the object they seek, are apt to move in the same way in other affairs of life; while those who zig-zag from side to side display the same lack of directness in business affairs and other activities of life. In the same way, one who makes short-cuts across corners, etc., is held to have the same tendency in active affairs.

Approbativeness shows itself in a strutting walk; while Self-Esteem manifests in a dignified carriage. Deficient, Self-Esteem shows itself in a cringing walk; while strong Reverence produces a respectful, deferential carriage. Approbativeness causes a slight swagger, with a defiant carriage of the head, while Combativeness manifests in a "get out of my way" pushing walk, the head being slightly lowered as if to "butt" a way through. Cunning manifests in a foxy, sly walk; while Cautiousness shows in a timid, hesitating step; and Acquisitiveness in a general carefulness and watchfulness as manifested in gait. A combination of Cunning, Cautiousness and Acquisitiveness, which is quite common, manifests in a light, stealthy step, giving the suggestion of "tip-toeing," and in extreme cases may show even the "snaky" gliding motion from side to side, in noiseless progression.

A little study and observation will convince anyone that the walk and carriage of an individual correspond very closely to his general character. And just as we may recognize one's mental characteristics when reproduced in outer form in the walk; so may we deduce the existence of mental characteristics in a stranger, from the outer form of his walk and carriage. The study of walk and carriage is very interesting, and will repay one for the time and trouble expended upon it. One may practice by observing the walk of an individual whose character is known, for the purpose of seeing the outer form of these characteristics; and also by observing the walk of those whose characters are unknown, and endeavoring to form an idea of their mental states and characteristics by means of their peculiarities of gait and carriage. One will be astonished at the proficiency attained in a short time by a little practice along these lines.

VOICE

The Voice is a great revealer of character. Prof. O. S. Fowler says: "Whatever makes a noise, from the deafening roar of sea, cataract, and whirlwind's mighty crash, through all forms of animal life, to the sweet and gentle voice of woman, makes a sound which agrees perfectly with the maker's character. Thus the terrific roar of the lion, and the soft cooing of the dove, correspond exactly with their respective dispositions; while the rough and powerful bellow of the bull, the fierce yell of the tiger, the coarse, guttural moan of the hyena, the swinish grunt, the sweet warblings of birds, in contrast with the raven's croak and the owl's hoot, each correspond perfectly with their respective characteristics. And this law holds equally true of man. Hence human intonations are as superior to brutal as human character exceeds animal. Accordingly, the peculiarities of all human beings are expressed in their voices and mode of speaking. Coarse-grained and powerful animal organizations have a coarse, harsh and grating voice, while in exact proportion as persons become refined and elevated mentally, will their tones of voice become correspondingly refined and perfected."

Prof. L. A. Vaught says: "Affectionate voices always come from the backhead. Heavy, thunderous voices always come from the sidehead. Egotistical voices come from the crown of the head. Kind, respectful and straightforward voices come from the tophead."

A clear, distinct utterance is held to indicate clear, logical thought, while indistinct, confused, slurring utterance is indicative of careless, illogical and hasty thought processes. Sharp and shrill notes denote nervous tension and lack of restraint, as witness the voice of the shrew or the hysterical woman, or the high-strung nervous man. Self-restraint is shown by calm, deep, forceful utterances. Slowness in delivery denotes slow, deliberate mental processes, while quickness, and "snappiness" in speech, denotes quick, active habits of thought. The cheerful voice of the optimistic person, and the rasping whine of the chronic pessimist, are well known. The voice of self-reliance, and the voice of fear and lack of self-esteem, are easily recognized. The strident, overconfident note of the boaster and vain-glorious person, is easily distinguished from that of the modest, careful, reliable person.

All the several mental Qualities manifest in the voice, in tone, pitch or feeling. The Emotive Qualities give the affectionate voice; Self-Esteem gives the confident voice; Approbativeness gives the voice of affectation and conceit; Combativeness gives the "let me alone" tone; Destructiveness gives the "get out of my way" note; Cunning and Acquisitiveness give the tone of deceit and flattery; and so on, through the entire scale. In studying voices it will help you to ask "What Quality or Qualities produce this voice?" in each case. Study the voices of those whose characteristics you know, and then apply the experience to others whose characteristics are unknown.

LAUGHS

Laughter is full of the expression of character. One may often accurately determine the character of a person whose face is not seen or known. A hearty laugh is indicative of sympathy, companionship and general sociability, as well as a well developed sense of humor. A giggle is indicative of pettiness, trifling and general mental light-weight. The repressed laugh shows self-control and often caution and cunning, the tone denoting the difference. The vulgar "haw-haw" denotes a correspondingly gross nature. The peculiar shrill, rasping, parrot-like laugh of the courtesan is typical, and when ever heard should act as a note of warning. It is difficult to state in words the various qualities of the laugh, but each is distinctive and well expresses the Quality causing it. It may be said that each and every mental Quality has its corresponding note in the laugh, which note may be learned and recognized by a little practice and actual observation.

THE HAND-SHAKE

The manner of shaking hands is indicative of the characteristics of the individual. Handshakes may be divided into three general classes, viz, (1) the hearty handshake, which indicates good-feeling, earnestness, and interest; (2) the mechanical handshake, which denotes indifference, lack of feeling, and lack of interest; and (3) the selfish handshake, which denotes cunning, heartlessness, and desire and disposition to take advantage of the other party. There is a "something" in the handshake which is almost impossible to express in words, but which is recognized instinctively by those having Human Nature well developed. It is more of a "feeling" of certain Qualities manifested by the other person. A little thought and attention paid to this subject will tend to develop this recognition on the part of one deficient in it. One may, with a little practice, learn to distinguish between the honest and the dishonest; the moral and the immoral; the active and the passive; the energetic and the slothful; the grasp of good-fellowship, and that of superciliousness; the friendly and the antagonistic; the candid and the deceitful; and all the other various kinds of handshakes. Mental states manifest in outer form in handshakes as in many other physical actions and appearances.

First study the several Qualities in their inner aspect, and then learn to distinguish the various outer forms of each. From the inner proceed to the outer, and having learned the way you will be able to retrace your steps from the outer to the inner in the case of other persons. The principle once grasped, the rest is all a matter of practice and experience.

FINIS.

Published by

Facsimile Publisher
Ashok Vihar, Delhi-110052 (India)
Website: www.facsimilepublisher.com

Distributed by

Gyan Books Pvt. Ltd.
5, Ansari Road, Daryaganj, New Delhi-110002 (India)
E-mail: books@gyanbooks.com, Website: www.gyanbooks.com

2 222000 010928